RAISING CHICKENS

A Step-by-Step Guide for Beginners

By Jason Howard

outlined in this book.

By reading this document, the reader agrees that under no circumstances is the author responsible for any losses, direct or indirect, which are incurred as a result of the use of information contained within this document, including, but not limited to, — errors, omissions, or inaccuracies.

Table of Contents

INTRODUCTION

If you're curious about what it takes to raise chickens in your backyard, you're not alone, and you've come to the right place!

According to the US Department of Agriculture, in 2014, one percent of people living in urban areas were raising chickens! That's 13 million people! And four percent more planned to add chickens to their life within the next five years.

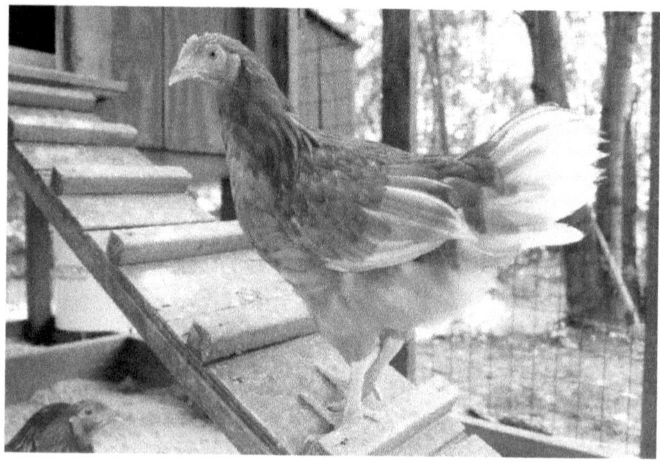

People raise chickens for lots of reasons. Chickens are known to be friendly, curious and social, so they make good pets. And, there's the delicious, fresh eggs they produce; you can eat them and also sell them. Some people compost chicken manure to use on their gardens. And, chickens provide natural pest control because they eat bugs. And some, when their hens stop laying, use their chickens for food. For all of these reasons, many find raising chickens really rewarding

So, you just buy a coop and some feed, buy some chickens and wait for the eggs, right?

Well, it's not that easy. But there's no need to worry – you'll get the inside scoop on chicken coops (including advice about building your own), types of chickens, where to buy them, daily, monthly and semi-yearly tasks, how to feed them, the ins-and-outs of incubation, how to gather and clean eggs, and how to keep your chickens happy and healthy. There's even some chicken stories from experienced owners.

Are chickens right for you? There's only one way to find out...

Grab your favorite beverage and a comfy chair, and let's learn all about raising chickens!

CHAPTER ONE

CHOOSING THE RIGHT CHICKEN COOP

Why a chicken coop? Your chickens will need a place to live, and some cities even require you to have a chicken coop. Even if you eventually want to go free range, you need something to protect your chickens and create a safe place for them at night. If you plan to raise chicks, the hens will need somewhere to sit on them. And, it's much easier to collect eggs. You can buy a simple or fancy coop or build your own. Some cities even have chicken coop building contests! Choosing the right coop and deciding whether to build or buy requires careful thought, though

Chickens should be let out of the coop during the day, and locked in at night. As with almost everything, people have their own ideas, so there's a bit of controversy about chicken coops. There's the "fresh air school" of chicken raising, which believes that chickens are harmed by confinement, bad air quality and the dark. This school of thought believes that the birds need an open-sided coop that makes conditions more like the outdoors. Others believe that chickens are more likely to get ill in the outdoors, and so they need an environmentally-controlled coop.

So, you'll see two basic designs: Houses with wide openings and nothing but chicken wire between the flock and the weather, and closed coops with windows, doors and hatches that can be closed. It doesn't matter which design you pick. Experts agree that ventilation is really important; you don't want heat stress or stroke, or for toxic fumes to build; all of these things can harm your flock.

Essential Considerations

Once you've decided you really want to raise chickens, your first step is to contact your local government to find out if backyard chickens are allowed and the rules and regulations. You wouldn't want to arrive home over the weekend with a beautiful new coop only to find that you have to take it back on Monday. And some governments require you purchase a permit.

Local laws may say that a coop has to be a certain distance from a house or other structures, such as schools, churches, etc.. Or, there's a limit on the number of chickens, or a prohibition on roosters. Unless you live on acreage, you're probably not allowed to have a rooster due to noise considerations. Check with your city zoning and code offices. And, if you rent, check with your landlord. If you have an HOA, check those rules as well. It's also probably a good idea to let your neighbors know what you're planning, especially if you're allowed to, and plan on, having a rooster.

Step two is to figure out how many chickens you want, and this, of course, will determine the size of the coop. The rule-of-thumb per the Old Farmer's Almanac, is to have two square feet of floor space per bird. You don't want to crowd the birds; not only will they be unhappy, but it's easier for disease to spread. And don't forget that they'll need some outdoor space, referred to as a chicken run. Similar to a kennel for dogs, it's an enclosed open-air space where they'll spend most of their day and where you'll feed your chickens.

What about bird breeds? Step three is choosing the chickens! The Old Farmer's Almanac cautions that some chickens have special needs, so for the beginning owner, your best bet is to choose varieties that thrive in all climates. After you have some experience under your belt, you can explore breeds like the Phoenix and Minorcas–they love the heat, or Brahmas and Chanteclers, which like it cool. Chapter Three will give you all the information you need to pick out the perfect chickens, but back to the subject of coops…

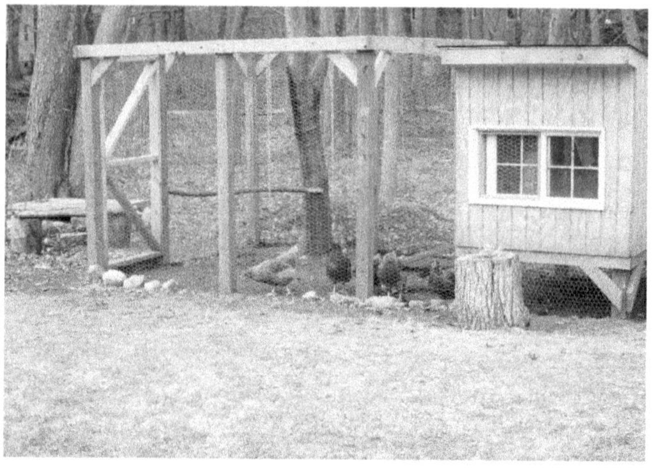

Predators. That word strikes fear into the heart of any backyard chicken farmer. Lots of animals, including domestic dogs and cats, love to chase, kill and eat chickens. To keep your chickens safe and happy, The Happy Chicken Coop and Grit websites offer the following tips:

- Do you know your local predators? Do you have raccoons, foxes, coyotes or skunks? What about snakes and large birds of prey? Are there a lot of feral cats or off-leash dogs? Knowing the predators is important for their control.
- You may want to create an underground barrier. Bury hardware mesh at least two feet deep, although four feet is better. Don't use

chicken wire–that's to keep chickens in, but doesn't work well to keep predators from digging. You want to keep animals from digging their way under your coop.

- Use fine-gauge chicken wire, or use two layers at angles to each other to keep predators from reaching into the coop. Use this technique for your run as well.
- If you live somewhere with a lot of hawks and owls, the chicken wire should keep them from grabbing a chick or even a full-grown hen. This will keep birds of prey out, but will allow light and air for your chickens.
- Cut down any large plants or vegetation that grows within 50-to-75 feet of your coop; this will give predators one less place to hide.
- Check your coop regularly for access holes. Wily predators can slither in. And don't pass over small openings–a weasel can get in through a half-inch hole. Weasels seem to kill for fun and you can lose all of your chickens in a single night.
- Make sure to lock your coop at night, and make sure your lock can't be opened by a critter like a raccoon with their little hands–they are quite smart! The Happy Chicken Coop recommends one that requires opposable thumbs. Also, use a padlock to keep

out people. Sadly, human chicken thieves can do as much damage as any wild animal.

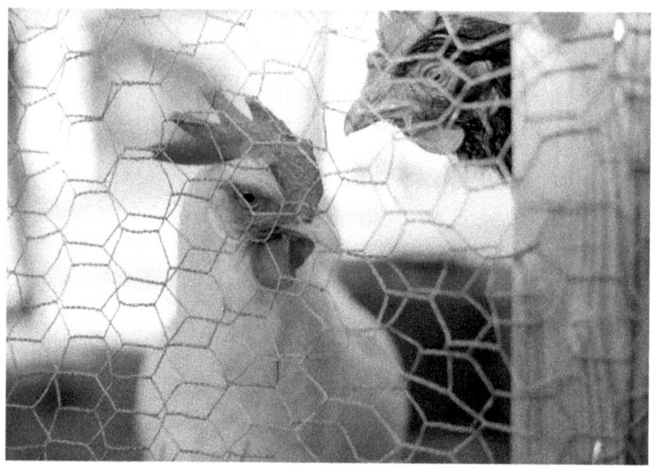

- Keep things clean. Food scraps will attract rats, which will eat chicks and eggs.
- Use lights that have a motion sensor. Many predators will be scared away by bright lights.
- Train your flock to return to the coop at night, and be sure to lock it. If chicks are raised in the coop, the hens will return to the coop to roost and lay eggs at night.
- Raise the coop about a foot or so off the ground so rats, skunks and snakes won't decide to live under the coop.
- Take swift action if you discover predator infiltration. If you don't stop things immediately, you'll just lose more chickens.

Weasels seem to kill for fun and you can lose all of your chickens in a single night. -thehappychickencoop.com

Now, let's talk about the budget for your chicken coop. Once you've decided how many chickens you have appropriate space for, decide how much you can spend. Keep in mind that buying the coop is just the start. You'll need waterers, and a feed trough big enough so all of your birds can feed at the same time. You'll also need enough pine wood shavings or straw for a six-inch floor layer, along with a few handfuls in each nest box. This will all be explored more in the following section on purchasing or building your coop.

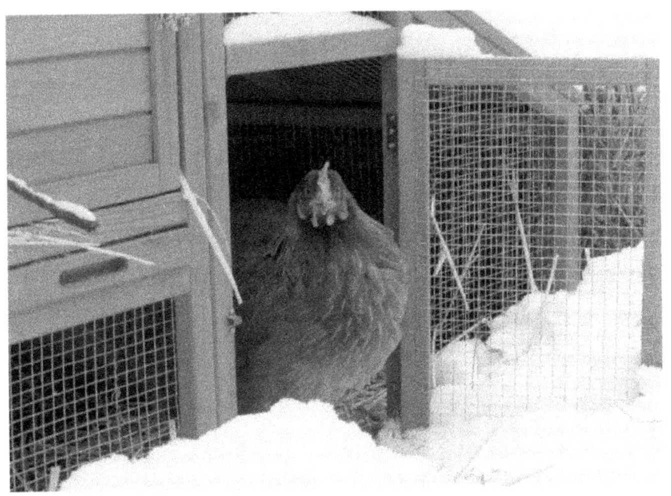

What about your climate? Heating chicken coops is a complicated issue. Some experts say that a properly managed coop doesn't need to be heated. The website Backyard Poultry recommends making sure your coop in winter is around 40 degrees fahrenheit if you're not brooding chicks, so your birds are comfortable and their water doesn't freeze. You'll read later about how important water is for chickens. But chickens are actually pretty good at surviving harsh conditions. If you give them a perch without a breeze, they can puff up their feathers to create an air gap between their skin and their feathers, which insulates them, and they fluff up enough to cover their feet and legs to prevent frostbite. You've probably seen photos of chickens with their heads tucked under their wing–they're keeping warm. You should also be sure your coop is well insulated to keep out cold and heat.

There are different types of chicken coop heaters, including flat panels, infrared heaters, and oil-filled radiator heaters. Under no circumstances should you use a heat lamp, no matter how safe the manufacturer says it is. A chicken could fly into it and catch it's feathers on fire and burn down the coop and incinerate the chickens. You'll see a lot of photos on the web with heat lamps because they are inexpensive, but they are not the safest option and are not recommended by experts or backyard chicken farmers.

The Community Chickens website also recommends not using a heat source that requires electricity unless you have a generator. If the electricity fails, chickens can die from sudden and extreme temperature drops. Use your own judgement on this; if you lose electrical service often in the winter, you might want to consider buying a generator. If not, you should have a plan for what to do if the power goes out and it's too cold for the birds. Be sure not to fatten your flock for the winter–like people, chickens are dying at incredible rates due to obesity.

But in your pursuit of ultimate chicken comfort, don't make your coop air-tight. Ventilation is needed to prevent moisture building up and lets out the ammonia formed by the bird waste. And bales of straw and hay can harbor mold and fungus. Another coop consideration is ease of use. Whether you buy or build a coop, as the "Dummies" website recommends, take these things into consideration:

- **Doors:** Make sure the doors are close enough to the nest boxes so they're easy to reach to gather eggs. Another door should allow access to food and water dishes, and be wide enough for you to take them out and put them into the coop. Make things easy on yourself and the flock.
- **Floor:** Some recommend wire floors with trays to collect waste, but most who keep

chickens feel this is difficult to walk on and uncomfortable to sit on. It also doesn't allow the bird to wear down their nails, so they can become overgrown, says the site My Pet Chicken. Plywood is a good material, and you will cover that with wood chips and straw. Do not use particle board, as it absorbs moisture.

- **Consider your property:** Some coops come on wheels so they are easy to move to different locations. This is great if you live somewhere that's flat, but if you're on a hill, that's probably not such a good thing! These coops on wheel are called chicken tractors, and you'll read about those in a bit.

Build Or Buy Your Coop?

Finding just the right coop for your chickens can be a daunting task. There are all sizes and shapes that come in easy-to-assemble kits. Then, there are free plans all over the web for DIY chicken coops. But should you build your first coop or buy one? The website ChickenCoop Design Plans recommends you ask yourself the following questions before making a decision:

1. **What is your budget?** Ready-made kits sell for hundreds, even thousands of dollars, depending on material quality and the size you need. And there is, of course, still assembly.

Constructing your own coop can cost about half of what you would pay for one ready-made, even if you buy all new materials. If you use recycled materials, you can save even more. Figure out if you can afford the cost of a new coop, and keep in mind that if you build your own, you get to choose the materials and the look.

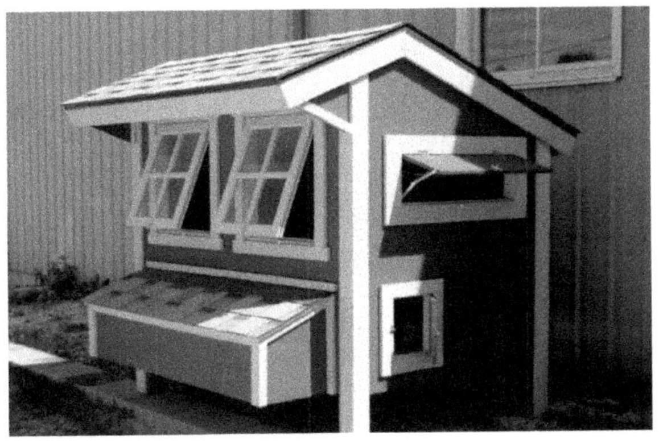

2. **Do you like DIY projects?** It can be fun and rewarding to build your own coop and see your design take shape. You'll feel a sense of pride every time you look at it. But is DIY for you? Be honest. Raising chickens, while it takes effort, should be fun. You don't want to look at your chickens every day and think about fingertip you cut off building their house!
3. **Do you have carpentry skills?** Again, be honest. If you have the ambition, but all you use a hammer for is to pound nails into a wall,

building your own chicken coop isn't something you'll want to tackle on your own. And, it's easy to be injured if you don't know what you're doing. Find a friend who's handy with tools and use your coop building as a learning experience. It also helps to have someone to hold things up and help you lift heavier pieces of wood. If you have older children, it can also be a great bonding experience.

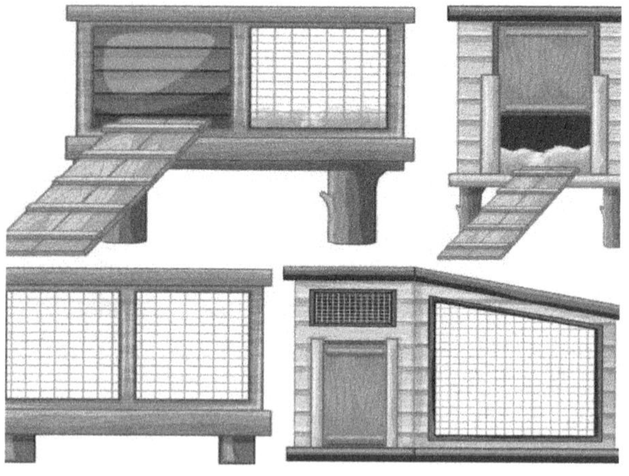

4. **Do you have the time?** If you plan on having just a few chickens, you can build your coop over a weekend. But if you plan on a larger flock, it can take months to build something large. Keep in mind that your coop has to be ready for when the chickens arrive, unless you're starting with chicks, which you'll likely

keep in your house in a box or pen for the first month.

1. **Custom coop requirements?** More than likely, if you've been thinking of getting chickens, you've been dreaming of how things will look. So, keeping that in mind, mull over where you want the house on your property and how you'll get the eggs. Is bending over an issue–do you need to be able to walk into the coop? Do you want to be able to get the eggs without going into the coop? Think about the weather to determine the number of ventilation vents–is where you live hot and humid? What about flooding? If water is a problem, you may have to use a concrete floor for your coop. And what about chicken exit and entry? Can they free range or do they need a run to be safe?
2. **Aesthetics?** Standard chicken houses usually are designed with a "country" look. Does that suit where you are? You'll probably want your coop to match the design of your home and landscaping. Building your own coop gives you plenty of design options.

Building or buying a coop is a big decision. Think carefully. If you decide to build your own coop, look at ready-made coops to find design features you like, and scour the web for design plans that you can either use as-is or modify to build your perfect chicken coop!

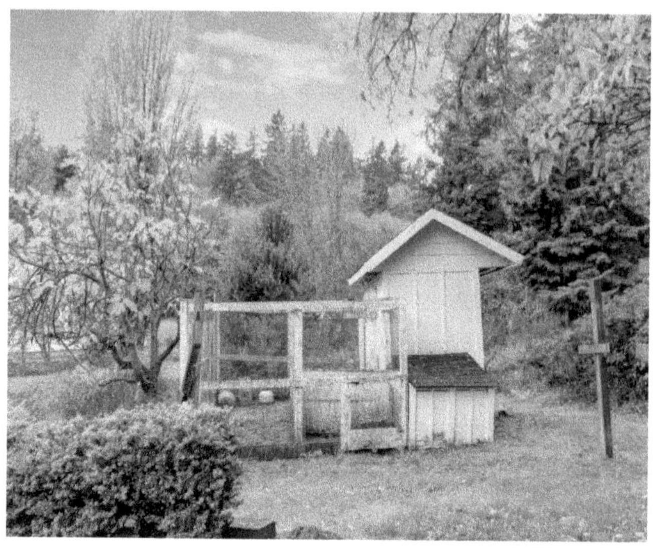

Whether you build or buy your chicken coop, you'll still need to kit it out, and you should make sure your design includes these must-have features:

- **Roost:** Chickens like sleeping in the air, and in the outdoors, chickens will sleep on a high place to avoid predators–wild chickens and domestic free range chickens will often sleep in trees. Sleeping on a roost also keeps the chickens off the floor. The roost should be made of wood, and positioned higher than the nesting boxes. Make sure your roost is sturdy, and long enough so all of your chickens can use it.

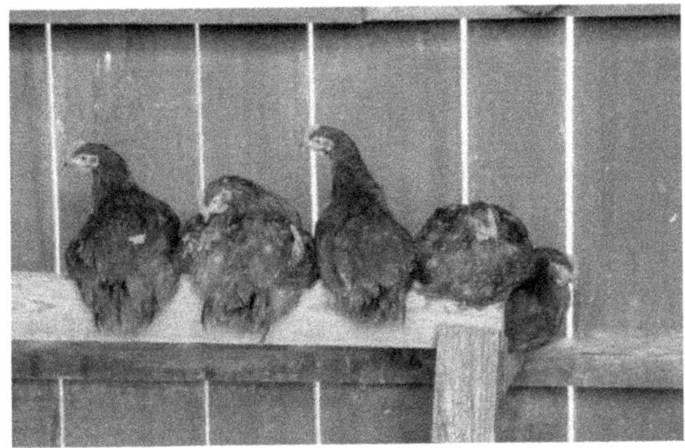

- **Nesting Boxes:** A nesting box is where your chickens lay eggs, which makes them easy to find when you want them. Keep the boxes as dark as possible and install them lower than the roosting bar. You should provide one box for every four-to-five chickens, and line them with dry bedding material like wood shavings or chopped straw, or whatever bedding material you choose.
- **Insulation:** Make sure your coop is well-ventilated, but make sure it's not drafty. And make sure to insulate the ceiling to help keep the coop cooler in summer. What kind of roof you use makes a difference, though. If you have a metal roof, you'll need to insulate between the metal and the framing. But, if

your coop has an asphalt shingle roof, if you use roof sheathing as a sun barrier, you won't need any additional insulation in the ceiling.

- **Lighting:** The reproductive cycle of a chicken are regulated by natural light, so if there's not enough, they may stop producing. Windows are ideal for the daytime, but artificial, low, yellow light is great for the winter. But don't have the lights on continuously, as it can affect reproductive cycles.
- **Ventilation:** Ammonia, released from fresh or moist chicken poop, can be bad for your chickens. Vents near the top of the coop will help remove contaminated air.
- **Litter trays:** Did you know that chickens poop while they sleep? Litter trays under the roost will help with clean-up. Make emptying the litter trays a part of your morning egg-collecting routine!
- **Raise the Floor:** The Hen House, a chicken coop manufacturer, recommends plywood for the floor, because it can be raised off the ground so there's airflow for less moisture, and it provides a tight floor against predators.
- **Food and Water:** Keep these away from the roost (see the litter tray above!) and you can suspend them off the ground a bit so they

don't collect as much bedding while the chickens are scratching.

- **Bedding:** Bedding goes on the floor and in the nesting boxes. There are many options, including:
  - **Sand:** It's inexpensive, but chicken mites like to live in it, so you would need to make sure you're treating your flock for mites.
  - **Shredded leaves:** You can shred these and use them in your coop; they help the poop compost into fertilizer. When you clean the coop, you can throw it into your garden.
  - **Cedar shavings:** These are easy to find at a feed store, help fight odor and can be composted. Pickup a dust mask when you buy your shavings, though; they can be very dusty.
  - **Pine shavings:** These absorb moisture, are readily available and also control odor.
  - **Paper:** Shred old bill and advertising flyers and put it on the floor and in nesting boxes. It isn't as good as cedar or pine, but it is free.
  - **Straw:** It's very common as bedding, but mites love to hide in it. If you use straw,

you'll need to sprinkle diatomaceous earth to defeat mites.

- **Hay:** It's more expensive than straw, but can be used as bedding.
- **Mulch:** You can often find free mulch from tree services–give them a call. The chickens love to scratch and poop in it, which makes mulch great for fertilizing your garden.
- **Sawdust:** If you live in an area with sawmill, sawdust makes great bedding, and absorbs moisture and waste.
- **Shredded cardboard:** You have to shred it, but you can use it on the floor and in the nesting boxes. This is another material you can use for garden compost.
- **Grass clippings:** Chickens are great fan of grass clippings. After you mow, collect the clippings and use them in your coop. Again, this makes great compost.

Some Coop Alternatives

Chicken Pen: As a less expensive option, a chicken pen might be just the thing for you, if it suits your weather. Also known as chicken runs, they can provide protection from predators while allowing your chickens to be outside. They are usually used with and attached to a coop, but a pen can be used alone.

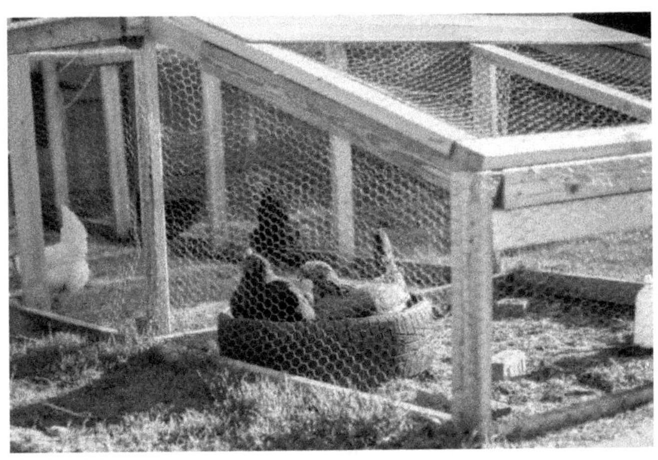

Unlike coops, which are solidly enclosed - pens are open on all sides and the top, using chicken wire to protect from predators. If you live somewhere with inclement weather, such as tornadoes or flash floods, you can make or buy a chicken pen that's portable, so you can move it, if necessary, to a safe location. It provides shelter, as well as food and a safe place for your flock to lay eggs.

You can buy or build pens; of course, building your own with recycled materials is going to be your cheapest option. Just remember that you want your pen to be easy to clean out, and clean it every one-to-two months at the most (remember, it's open-air, so there's no ammonia buildup) and you can use the chicken poop as fertilizer, and of course, lock up your pen at night for safety.

Chicken Tractors:

Chickens on wheels? If you have a large yard or acreage, a chicken tractor might be for you, says Modern Farmer! It's basically a coop on wheels.

The idea is that you move your chicken tractor across your yard every few days. This gives your flock constant fresh vegetation. Chickens love tender grass tips and weeds, and will also eat bugs, slugs and snails. And, as you move the tractor around, the chickens leave their manure behind, which makes a great fertilizer, rich in nitrogen and phosphorus.

Why is it called a tractor? Well, the scratching action of the birds rips up the vegetation and loosens the top inch or so of soil. Got a bunch of weeds and want to plant a garden in that spot? Put your chickens to work clearing the land for you. You'll have to leave the tractor in one place for a bit and then move it as they clear each space. If you just want pest control and fertilization without the resulting dirt patch, you should move the tractor daily.

There are lots of plans on the internet for chicken tractors, and they range from thrown-together ramshackle contraptions to beautiful tractors that repurpose things like old cars, mobile homes, school buses or equipment trailers. It's a great chance to use your imagination and ingenuity. But, if that isn't for you, you can buy a prefab units; prices start at about

$350 for a pretty basic model to over $2,000 for a fancy luxury tractor.

All chicken tractors have the same basic components: Enclosed nesting area, a run covered with wire mesh to keep out predators, and a frame with wheels. Just remember, if your property is sloped, a tractor probably isn't a good idea unless you want to chase it down a hill!

In this chapter, you learned about:

- Coops: What type? How big? Do you need heat? What about feeders and waterers? Roosts? Are you interested in building your own?
- Pens: Be sure to protect from predators by following the rules for wire and flooring.
- Number of chickens: Remember the rule about two square feet per bird.
- Bedding: Lots of choices there. Which one is best for you and easiest to get?
- Nest boxes: Location, location, location. You don't want them pooping in them.
- Cleaning up the area: You don't want cover for critters, plants that are poisonous or plants you want to keep that might be destroyed if they're too near the area.

Lots to think about and decide. Once you have your coop built or bought, and fully equipped, it's time to get the chickens. But which chickens? You'll get the chicken-picking guidance you need in the next chapter. This is the exciting part!

CHAPTER TWO

CHOOSING YOUR CHICKENS

Quiz question: How many breeds of chickens are there? Answer: No one knows! No one keeps track! Wikipedia says hundreds, and Professor C.J. Nichol of the University of London has counted more than 500 "fancy breeds" worldwide, described as ranging "from the sublime to the ridiculous."

The American Poultry Association recognizes 63 large chicken breeds and some additional bantam breeds (bantams are small chickens, usually one-quarter to one-fifth the size of standard). However, there are other breeds that this association doesn't recognize, including those that aren't well established in the United States (US), but are in their countries of origin, as well as some others that haven't made their way to the US yet.

So, with that many breeds, which chickens are best for the beginning chicken farmer?

Deciding on a Breed

As a beginner, picking the right breed of chicken is important. Pick the right one, and you want to spend your days hanging out with your flock; pick the wrong one and you'll wonder why, oh, why, you ever decided to raise chickens!

You might think that particular breed of chicken is cute, but is it really what you want or need? Ask yourself the following questions, provided by The Happy Chicken Coop:

1. Why do you want chickens? For eggs, pets, meat or a combination?
2. How much time do you expect to spend caring for your flock? Some breeds require more time and maintenance.
3. Is your weather and climate suitable for the breed you like? Most breeds are fine in all climates, and if you are buying them from a local supplier, they should be fine. But, if you're buying rare breeds (which aren't recommended until you have some experience under your belt), make very sure the climate works for them.
4. How much space can you give your chickens? Some breeds need more space than others, and if they don't get it they can

get violent, peck and attack each other. Match the breed to the space.

5. How about the budget? Most breeds cost about the same, but rare exotics can cost thousands of dollars! According to the Frugal Chicken website, as a general guideline: Baby chicks start at $1 each, with an average price of $5; age 4–16 weeks, about $15 to $25; and laying hens about $10 to $100, depending on the breed.

Chickens live for eight to ten years, and will usually lay eggs for seven years.

Best Chicken Breeds for Beginners

Most beginners want chickens that are easy to keep, great layers that are docile, and those that aren't very noisy.

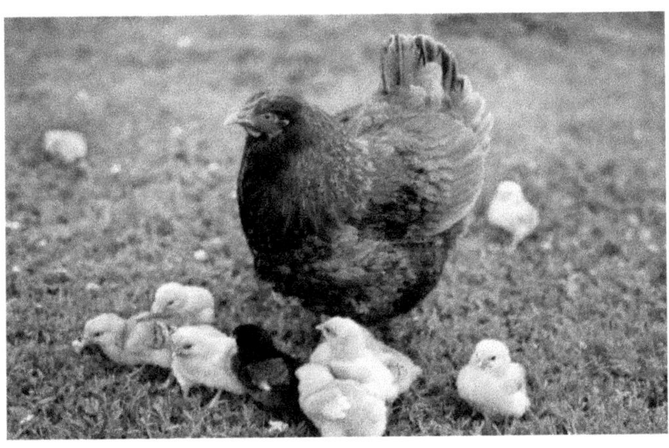

The best chicken breeds for those just getting started with chickens include:

Rhode Island Red

Rhode Island Reds date back to the late 1850's. They're exceptionally hardy and lay large brown eggs. As far as personality goes, some say they are easygoing, but others say their bossy. The Rhode Island Red is the state bird of Rhode Island! Many say these are their favorite chickens because of their great personality.

They're friendly, tough and easy to keep healthy, and they should produce more than 250 eggs per year. And, they lay all year around and don't require too much space.

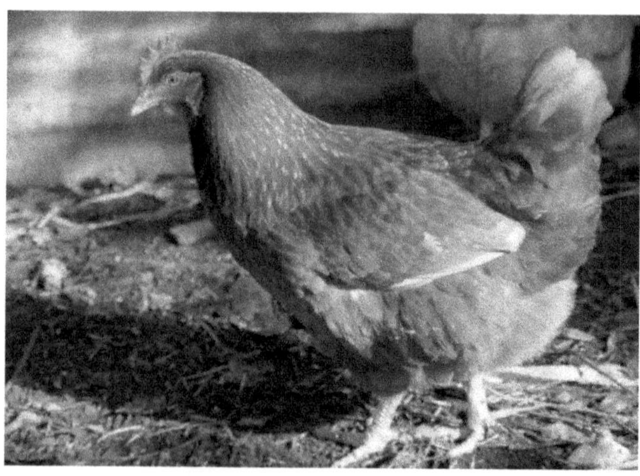

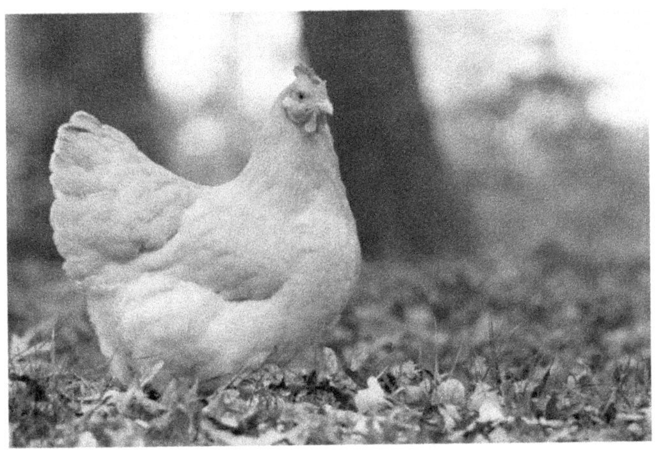

Hybrid

Hybrids, like the Golden Comet, are bred for a specific purpose–to consume small amounts of food and lay as many eggs as they possibly can. This might be great for you, but it's not great for the hen's health as their body never gets to rest unless the chicken is molting.

They can lay more than 280, medium-sized brown eggs per year, so they make a great choice. The thing to watch with hybrids is that they haven't been overbred; and be sure to buy from a sustainable breeder.

Buff Orpington

This particular chicken with the odd name originated in 1886 in Orpington, Kent, England. A coachman by the name of William Cook wanted to breed a better chicken–one that lays lots of eggs but is also good for the table. The first Orpingtons were black, but the buff color you see above was, and remains, the most popular.

These chickens are known for their sturdiness and good looks, and they make great pets because they're very friendly and very soft. They do get broody (meaning she wants to hatch eggs and raise chicks) so their egg production is lower than the Rhode Island Red and Hybrid–you can expect about 180 medium-sized, light brown eggs annually.

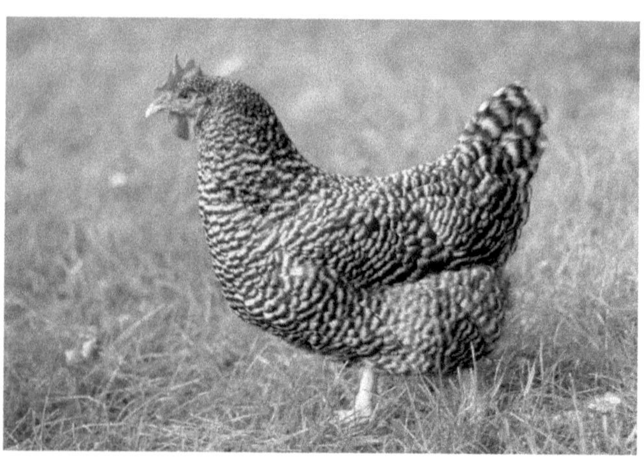

Plymouth Rock

The Plymouth Rock is renowned for being the United State's main source of chicken meat and eggs during World War II, and is one of America's oldest chicken breeds. When the chicken industry became mechanized, it was cast aside by commercial breeders who thought their egg production was too low.

This is an active bird that's extremely friendly. So much so that they are easily trained to eat out of your hand. They should produce 200, medium-sized brown-to-pink eggs each year, and they lay during the winter.

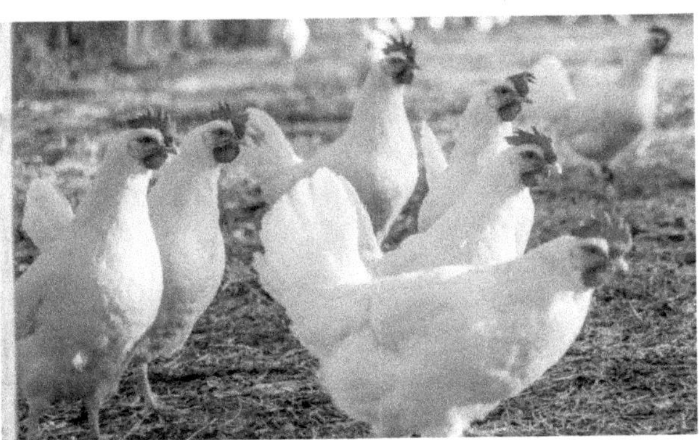

Leghorn

If you've ever seen those old Bugs Bunny cartoons with Foghorn Leghorn, you'll recognize the male chicken in this photo. The origin of the Leghorn is shrouded in mystery, and these snowy white birds were once called Italians, because they were bred from several small racing breeds in the Tuscany region of Italy.

Leghorns aren't good for pets because they're not very tame. They're very active, and should produce more than 250 medium-sized white eggs a year.

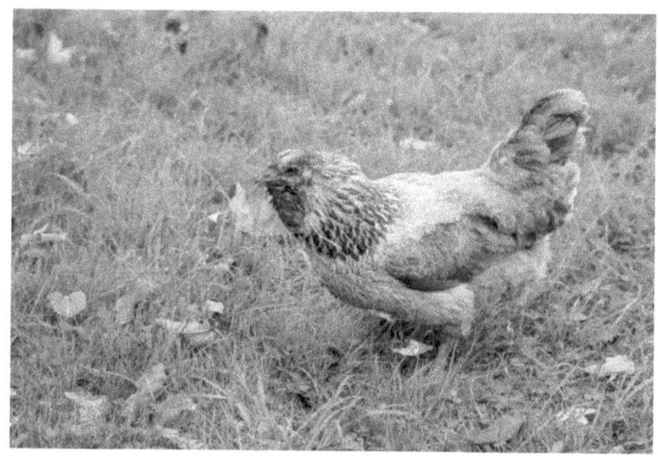

Ameraucana

Want some colored eggs? Ameraucana are a relatively new breed, appearing in the 1970s. They come in a number of colors, from black to white to blue to beige. They are an all-purpose (meaning they are used for eggs and meat), winter-hardy breed. They were developed in the United States from Araucana chickens from Chile. They keep the blue egg gene, but the lethal genes of ear-tufts and rumplessness have been bred out.

Ameraucana are friendly, but don't like to be picked up and handled. They will produce around 150 blue eggs per year.

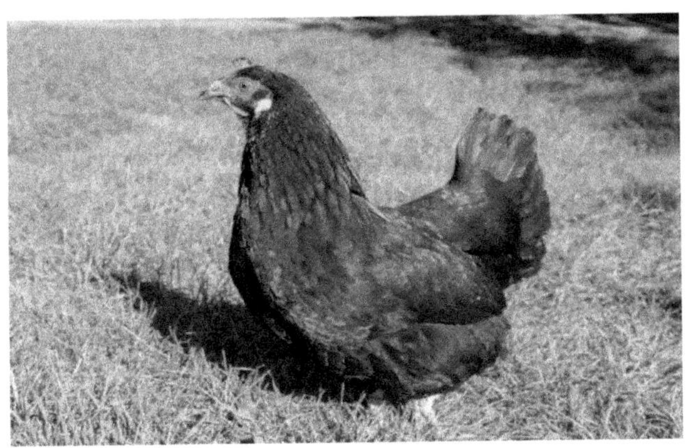

Australorp

Australorps are a calm and friendly breed, with soft, shiny black plumage that has hints of green and purple in the sun. They are known to be shy and quite sweet. As you might guess from their name, this breed originated in Australia.

They are dignified and peaceful, and they will lay over 250 brown eggs a year.

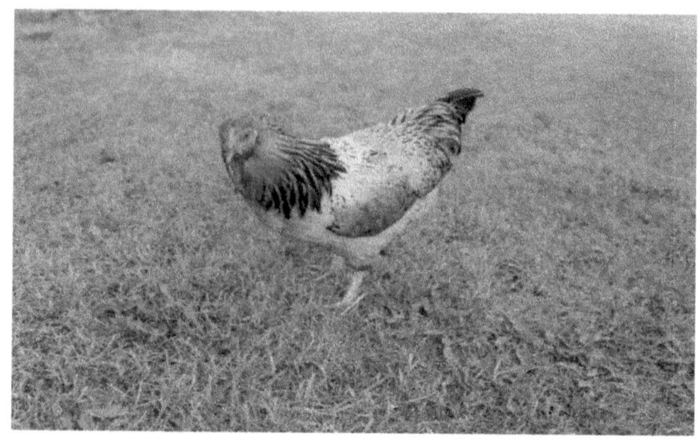

Easter Egger

If you have a hankering for colored eggs, an Easter Egger is for you. They aren't really a breed, because they don't conform to breed standards for the Ameraucana or Araucana chickens from whence they came, but they are charming hybrids. They vary a lot in appearance, and they lay green, blue or pink eggs.

These chickens are also called "rainbow layers" and they lay around 250 colored eggs a year.

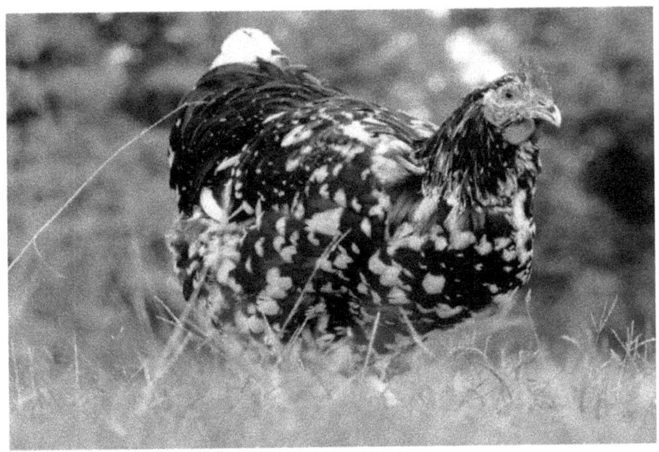

Sussex

The Sussex is a dual-purpose chicken (eggs and meat) thought to have originated in England at the time of the Roman invasion, but the breed and color refinement started during the Victorian era, when they were bred with Cochins, Dorking, Brahma and others. It was considered the finest of eating birds. They are docile, but friendly and confident, as well as incredibly curious.

They lay around 250 large brown eggs a week, and they lay year round.

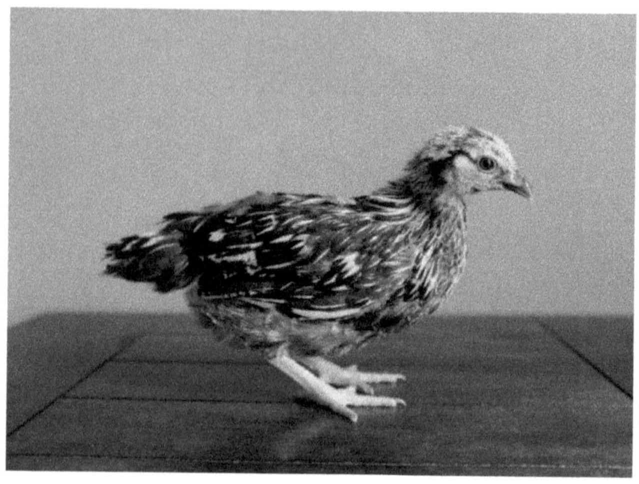

Wyandotte

The Wyandotte was created in the northeastern United States, and it's become one of America's favorite chickens. Itt was the first American breed specifically bred to be dual-purpose. The original name was American Sebright, but the name was changed to Wyandotte for the Wyandotte Indian Nation to honor the help they'd given white settlers. They come in 30 different colors. They have a dominant streak, which means they'll probably end up high in the pecking order. They love being fussed over and are child-friendly.

They lay about 200 medium-to-large brown eggs a year, and lay through the winter.

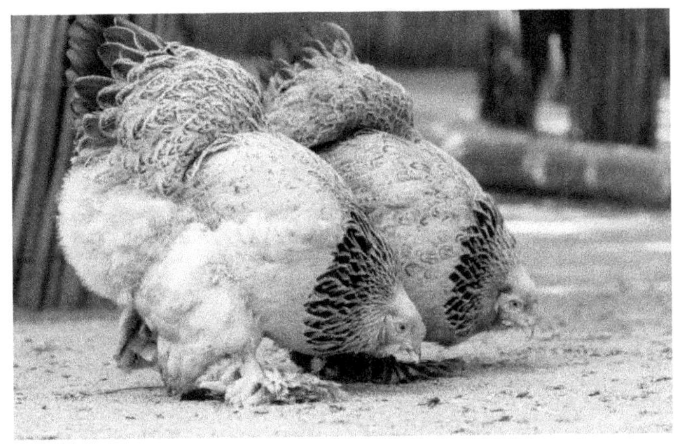

Brahma

The majestic and beautiful Brahma is an old breed, and it's exact genetic makeup is unknown, but it's believed the original birds came from China and were bred in India. It's a large bird, around 30 inches tall, but there's also a bantam variety. They are docile and calm dual-purpose chickens.

Brahmas prefer to lay from October until May, so they will be producing when other chickens stop for the winter. They will produce around 150 to 200 medium-to-large brown eggs annually.

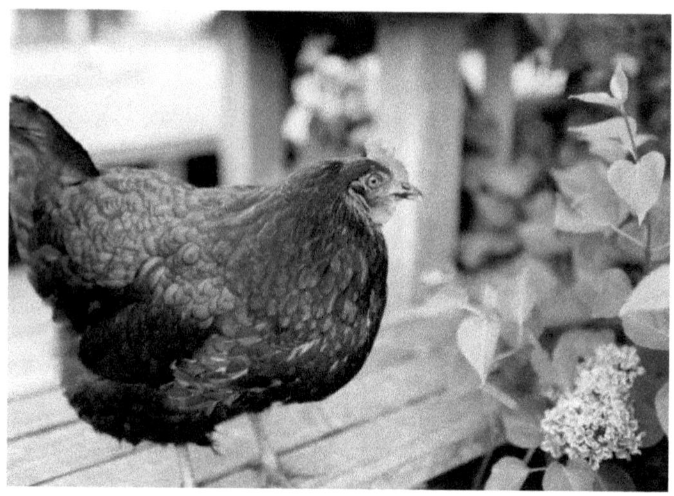

Jersey Giant

The Jersey Giant is the largest purebred chicken in the United States, and perhaps the world. The only other breed that comes close in size is the Brahma. They were originally developed–you guessed it–in New Jersey around the 1870s, when there was a demand for heavy roasting birds. They are a mix of Black Java, black Langshan and dark Brahma. They are a rare breed, and in 2001 were listed as critically endangered by the Livestock Conservancy. As of 2017, they've been moved to the watch list; backyard keepers are helping the Jersey Giant regain its popularity! It's a mellow, friendly bird and good with children.

The Jersey Giant lays around 150-to-200 very large, light-to-medium brown eggs per year. Where they really stand out is with meat production–one bird can easily feed a family of four. Be sure to collect eggs quickly; these large birds can crush them.

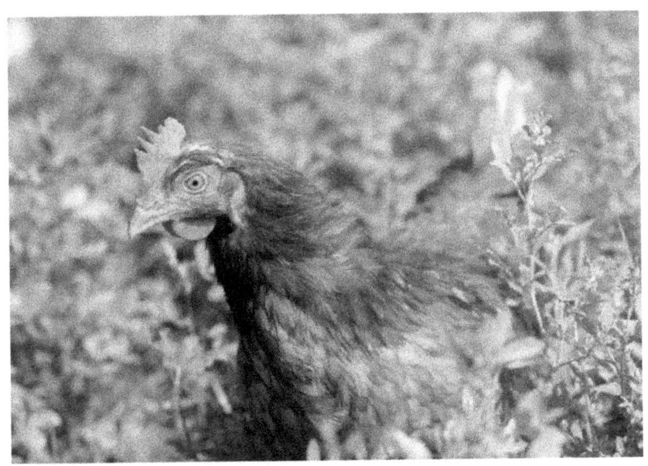

Red Star

Red Star chickens were originally created in the 1950s to lay huge amounts of eggs. It's not a breed, but a hybrid that's also known as Sex-Link and Golden Comet. It's often found, beside the Leghorn in commercial operations.

It's interesting that before this hybrid was developed, breeding "mutt" chickens was looked down upon. The Star changed all that. They are called "sex link" because two Star chickens will not produce other Red Stars. If you want your own Red Stars, breed Rhode Island Reds with White Rocks. Since it's a hybrid chicken, the colors vary based on the mated breeds.

These prolific hens lay 300-to-360 beautiful brown eggs a year.

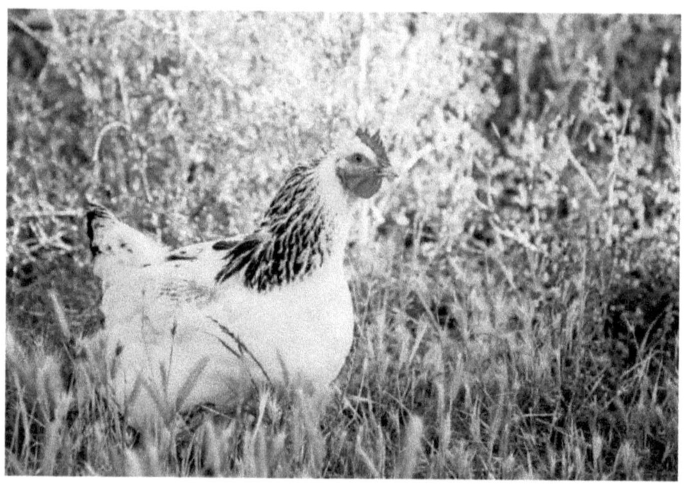

Delaware

The Delaware is a relatively new breed of chicken, and in the 1940s, it was hoped it would become the superstar of the broiler industry, but when that didn't happen, they fell into obscurity. The only reason they're around today is because of a few people who continued to keep the breed. They are calm, curious, friendly and intelligent. And, apparently, they love to "talk!"

Delawares will lay about 200 large-to-jumbo-sized eggs per year. They aren't broody, so if you want chicks, you'll have to use an incubator.

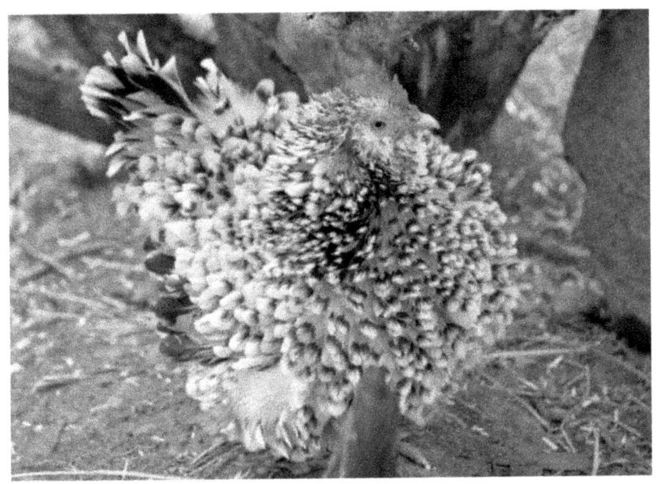

Belgian D'Uccle

Belgian d'Uccle chickens, also known as Barbu D'Uccles, are prized for their friendly, sweet, and cuddly personality. Owners report that they'll often fly up to your shoulder or arm, just to sit and chat. They're also very calm, although they can get a bit feisty during mating season.

This breed was created by a rich Dutch businessman, and it became popular fast. No one is sure exactly what breeds were used. They are known for being broody, and they make great mothers to any chicks, so they're great for hatching fertilized eggs. They'll sit on the eggs until they hatch, and then tend to the chicks.

They come in different colors, and add some glamor to a coop. They aren't great layers–maybe 150 eggs per year, but they make great pets.

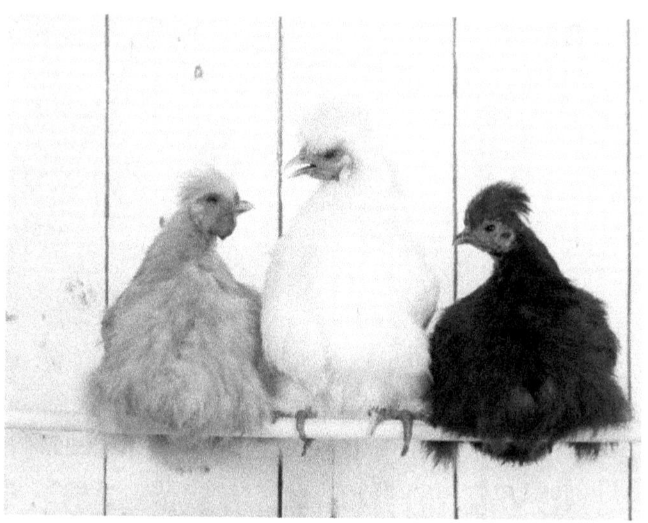

Silkie

Silkies are a small breed of chicken–a bantam, which you read earlier is one-quarter to one-fifth the size of a regular chicken. And Silkies aren't the greatest layers–only a bit over 150 eggs per year. And you have to keep them warm in winter, they can't get wet, and they need to be watched around bigger birds because they can get picked (and pecked) on. Plus, they have other special needs.

In spite of that, they are quite popular. Many chicken fans call them the "sweetest chickens ever."

They are great with kids, and are adorably fluffy, with feathers that feel like silk, hence their name. And they love to be stroked and snuggled. If you have children, or want a special chicken pet, you might want to consider adding a Silkie after you get more experience under your belt.

Just keep in mind that the Centers for Disease Control recommend not kissing chickens, and not to let them into your house due to the risk of salmonella.

What To Look For When Purchasing Chickens

Chickens of different age ranges are sold: Baby chicks, pullets, point of lay, and laying hens. The age of baby chicks is usually one day. They are quite delicate, and probably not a good bet for your first chickens. Later on, you'll read about hatching chicks of your own.

Pullets are around 10 weeks old, and have their adult feathers so they don't need heat to stay warm. Buying pullets is a great option because they're stronger, bigger and more independent, but young enough to form a bond with and train easily.

Point of lay hens are usually around 18 weeks to 20 weeks old and are at the point of laying their first eggs, although purebred hens usually need to be a few weeks older. They are considered adult birds at this stage and unless there's something breed-specific, they don't require any extra care.

Laying hens are in their first year or later of laying eggs. If you purchase an adult laying hen, expect to pay more, but you'll have fresh eggs right away. The seller should be able to tell you how many eggs it lays.

You've decided which breed of chicken and what age you'd like, but how do you know if you're getting a strong, healthy chicken? Know what to look for before you go chicken shopping.

How to Tell If The Bird Is Healthy

It's important to buy from a place that treats their animals well. It doesn't matter where you buy them; make sure they are well cared for and the facility is clean. And if you see any sick animals, animals living in filth or untreated wounds, turn around and walk away.

Check reviews if you're buying birds by mail order, and do as much research on the business as you possibly can. After all, you won't be there to see the chickens and how they're raised, so you'll be relying on the experience of other people. So that you can make an informed decision, read reviews carefully.

According to Backyard Chicken Project, healthy adult chickens share these traits:

- Nostrils: Make sure nostrils are clean and clear with no discharge or fluid.
- Eyes: Look into their eyes. Are they bright and clear with no swollen or bright red skin around them? There should be no discharge, the eyes shouldn't droop, and the chicken shouldn't be excessively blinking
- Legs: Chicken have scales on their legs, and they should be smooth with flat plates, no odd coloring or wounds.
- Feet: Are the bottom of the feet free from wounds or infections? Looking at the top of the feet, the nails should lay flat against the toes and shouldn't be crooked or too long.
- Feathers: If you're buying an adult bird, the feathers should be smooth and flat, or dry and fluffy when buying a chick. Mites and lice often create bald spots, so examine the chicken carefully to check there aren't any spots without feathers.
- Beak: The beak should be even and close fully, and the top and bottom beaks shouldn't be bent or broken.
- Stature: Your potential chicken should be able to stand without limping, stand tall, and the neck should be strong. Be sure the head isn't drooping, and the bird has no body quakes and shaking.

- Sounds: There should be no rattling sounds, wheezing, coughing or sneezing.
- Muscle: Very prominent breast bones are a sign of underweight, so check the muscle on both sides of the bones.

When buying chicks, in addition to checking all of the above, make sure they are bright eyed, playful and energetic.

Note: If you buy from a National Poultry Improvement Plan,
chickens are tested for disease yearly,
and the place you're buying is inspected by a state veterinarian,
you most likely will not be able to visit the chicks or pens due to biosecurity rules
--backyardchickens.com

If the chickens you want to buy only have a couple of these signs, you could take them home and nurse them back to health, but if you are adding to your flock, keep in mind that you should quarantine the new bird for three weeks to make sure they don't have something that can infect the other chickens.

How to Tell Males from Females

When chickens are over five months old, it's easy to tell males from females, but when they're young, they don't have the adult characteristics (such as a

Rooster's comb) that make it easy to judge. So just what do you look for?

First things first: Pullets are female chickens and cockerels are male chickens.

At one week old: Pullets have wing and tail feathers developing, while males likely do not.

At five weeks old:

- Cockerels are bigger than pullets
- While both have combs, the cockerel's is bigger and redder
- Cockerels are friendlier and braver
- Long, thick legs mean it's a cockerel
- Cockerels have a curved tail that's stumpy
- You'll see less developed feathering in cockerels, including on the back, legs, side of the neck, crops, and wings.

One great trick to tell the sex of a chicken comes from Backyard Chickens: Put your finger in front of the chicken's face/beak. Cockerels will stand up to you and pullets cower down.

Are They Good Laying Hens?

Make sure your hens are at the right age for laying eggs, and look for active birds that are bright eyed and bright red combs. Pass up the ones that look depressed or dull.

You want to look for a bird that is actively laying. These hens will have hip bones widely spaced and the breastbone will be tilted downward–these changes to the bird's body give more room for egg development in the abdomen.

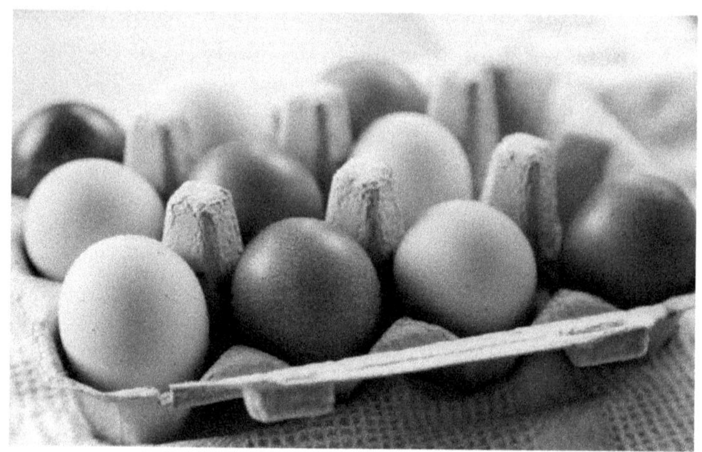

Some Breeds Lay Colored Eggs

If you've been buying eggs from the grocery store, you probably don't realize that eggs come in a variety of colors, depending on the breed of chicken. If you've been buying from a local farmer or backyard chicken fancier, you might have seen them. Come Easter, there's no need to dye eggs with these eggs! So, which bird lays which color?

Light tan eggs: Buff Orpington, Lavender Orpington, Laced/Silver Laced Wyandotte, Speckled Sussex.

White eggs: Andalusian, Belgian D'Uccle, Campine, Catalana, Hamburg, Lakenvelder, Leghorn, Minorca, Polish, Russian Orloff, Sabelpoot, Sebright, Sicilian Buttercup, Silkie, White Faced Black Spanish.

Cream eggs: Dorking, Easter Egger (some), Faverolle.

Pink eggs: Asil, Australorps (some), Easter Eggers (some), Langshan, Light Sussex, Plymouth Rock.

Chocolate Brown eggs: Barnvelder, Black/Blue Copper Marans, Penedesenca.

Speckled eggs: Cuckoo Marans, Welsummer

Green eggs: Easter Eggers (some), Ice Cream Bar, Isbar, Olive Eggers.

Blue eggs: Ameraucana, Araucana, Cream Legbar, Easter Egger (some).

If you like surprises, add some Easter Eggers to your flock. They can lay a variety of shades of green, pinkish or cream eggs. Each hen will only lay one color egg in her life, but each Easter Eggers can lay a different color egg. It's a complete mystery until she lays her first egg!

But why are chicken eggs different colors? Michigan State University Extension has the answer!

First of all, the color of the egg has no impact on its nutritional value, even though public perception is that brown eggs are healthier than white eggs.

Egg color is decided by hen genetics, so the breed of hen will determine which color eggs she'll produce. Some colors are produced by cross-breeding. For example, an Olive Egger, which produces olive green eggs, is a cross between a hen and rooster that are from a brown egg and blue egg breed.

Interesting tip: Look at the hen's ear lobes. Usually those with white earlobes lay white eggs.

-Michigan State University Extension

All eggs start out white. Colored eggs have pigments deposited on the shell as they move through the hen's oviduct (a tube-like organ where the egg finishes developing). The pigment penetrates the egg shell, which means the interior and exterior of the shell are the same color. But, chickens that produce brown eggs deposit a pigment on the eggs late in the formation of the shell, so it doesn't penetrate the interior, which is why you don't see brown egg whites.

Where to Purchase Chickens

You've decided which breed or breeds you'd like to start with. But, where do you get chickens? There are a number of good sources.

You can buy chickens online or by mail order. Use your search engine to look for hatcheries. Most hatcheries ship with a guarantee that your chickens will arrive alive and well, but be sure to check all store policies before you order.

Local farms often have chickens, and when you buy from a local farmer, you know those chickens are right for your climate. Check your local newspaper and ask around about local farms that sell chicks.

Animal shelters, believe it or not, can be a source for chickens. Check with your local shelters and rescues to see if they have chickens or if there is a specialized livestock shelter near you.

Farm stores and feed stores usually have chicks for sale in the spring. They won't carry as many breeds as a mail order supplier, but that means the chickens will be less stressed when they get to their new home.

You also can check Craigslist and similar sites, but be very careful. The Backyard Chicken Project warns that there are many reasons why people might sell chickens on Craigslist, and not all of them are good.

The birds may be sick, they may have bad behavior or they could be from bad breeding stock and have health problems in the future. Ask a lot of questions and make sure to spend some time with the birds.

What about Roosters?

Deciding to keep a rooster is a big decision. Your first step is to check with your local government. Are you even allowed to have a rooster? And don't think you can get one and hide it–roosters can be noisy! So, check with your neighbors as well. If the houses are far enough apart, they may not hear the crowing unless they're outside.

Why would you have a rooster? Well, if you like to eat fertilized eggs and hatch your own chicks, it's a necessity. They offer protection to the flock be alerting them to predators, and when they find something delicious to eat, a rooster will call his hens to have some.

But… Roosters crow at the crack of dawn as well as throughout the day. And don't consider getting a rooster if you have fewer than eight hens. Your virile rooster will mate regularly with all of his hens, and if you don't have enough hens to divide his time, the rooster could wear them out and cause damage to their combs, necks and backs from his beak and spurs. A good minimum is eight-to-ten hens per rooster.

But don't worry, hens will lay nutritious eggs without their male counterpart.

You've picked your chicken breeds, learned how to choose healthy birds and learned where you can buy them. Oh, and a bit about roosters too. But just how do you take care of them? The next chapter outlines what to do when for the ultimate in chicken care.

CHAPTER THREE

CHICKEN CARE: DAILY, WEEKLY, MONTHLY AND SEMI-YEARLY TASKS

As you've probably figured out by now, there's more to raising chickens than giving them a place to live. There are things you must do daily (many are obvious, but all are important) or monthly chores and tasks that need doing only twice a year.

Most of these chicken-care tasks apply to all chicken farmers. However, if you decide later to go free-range, of course some things you wouldn't do, like let your chickens out into the run. And, if you use a tractor coop and want to fertilize rather than devegetate your land, you'll have to move your coop every day.

Necessary Equipment

Later on, you'll learn about feeders and waterers, as well as food. The tools we're talking about here are things that will help you clean your coop and outdoor areas, courtesy of Backyard Chicken Coops.

- **Garden Hoe:** Use it to scrape off the roost and pull dirty bedding from nesting boxes.
- **Small Shovel or Cat Litter Scoop:** To get poop out of the coop
- **Rake or Shovel:** Also helps remove bedding
- **Paint Scraper:** Scrape up stick poop residue
- **Wheelbarrow:** To carry soiled bedding to the compost heap if you have a large flock
- **Muck Bucket:** You'll put the chicken poop in here. If you have a compost pile, you'll add any human food waste to this bucket before putting it on your compost pile. This bucket should *only* be used for transporting poop and soiled bedding.
- **Broom:** Great for coaxing dawdling birds into the coop at night.
- **Basket or Bucket for egg collection**
- **Egg-count Journal:** Write down how many eggs you get a day, if you like.
- **Thermometer:** If you live somewhere that gets really hot or really cold, be sure to hang a thermometer in the coop.
- **Small feed bucket:** For daily feeding

- **Large, Secure Feed Container and Scoop:** You'll store feed here so that rats and other animals can't get into it.
- **Dust Mask:** Use this when cleaning out the coop to avoid breathing in dust or anything harmful in the air.
- **Disinfectant:** White vinegar works well. Be sure to scrub, scrub, scrub. Do not use bleach or any kind of household disinfectant.
- **Scrub Brush:** For deep cleaning your coop.

Okay, you have your list, you've bought your tools, so let's talk about what you'll be doing with them! These are rough guidelines – you may have to do monthly chores more often – just keep an eye on things and use your best judgement.

Daily Tasks:

- If you compost, grab your food scraps and head out into the yard. Open the coop and let the chickens out into their run, if weather permits.
- Scrape the roost, and clean the floor of the coop (and the nesting boxes if necessary). Put the chicken poop into your muck bucket, and add the kitchen scraps. Take the bucket to your compost pile. If you don't compost, toss into the garbage.

- Feed your chickens. You'll read more about types of food, etc. Chickens should have a constant supply of food
    - **You'll want to collect eggs every morning; hens cackling loudly are a sign or clue that they're laying. I usually have another look in the afternoon, as well.**
    - **-The Old Farmer's Almanac**
- Collect eggs, and fill in your egg journal if you keep one. You want to collect eggs a couple of times a day for a number of reasons: They stay cleaner. And chickens can break them; chickens also eat eggs. The Old Farmer's Almanac says most egg-eating chickens start out eating a broken egg, and then will break eggs themselves so they can feast. Remember, chickens will pick at anything that looks edible.
- Rake and tidy up bedding – remove the dirtiest and add clean bedding.
- Do a quick health check. Hang out with your flock. Are they are alert, bright-eyed and active? This is your chance to catch any health problems early.
- If you have a thermometer in your coop, check it and take action if necessary.
- Provide some treats sometime during the day.

- When it's dusk, get the chickens back into their coop (this is where the broom can come in handy) and close all doors and gates securely. Make sure they have ventilation.

Weekly Tasks

- Clean and tidy the coop and rake out and replace the bedding. This helps keep moisture and pests at bay. Moisture lets bacteria grow.
- Refill grit and oyster shells – you'll read more about this later, but these are two essential supplements for chickens so they can digest their food properly and make strong egg shells. Your chickens will need a constant supply of both of these so they can just take what they need.
- Rake your chicken run. Remove waste and any wet and dirty material. A dirty run can mean a buildup of moisture and chicken waste that creates an unhealthy environment.

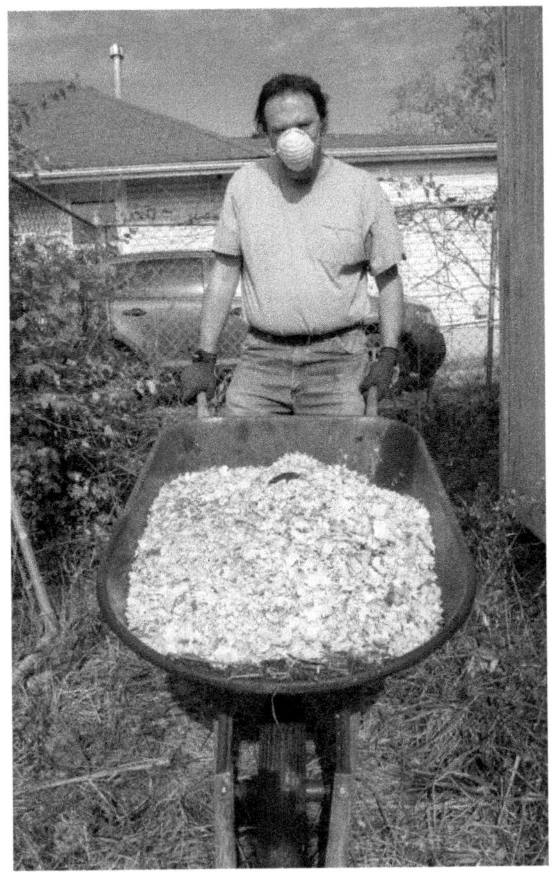

Monthly Tasks

- Replenish feed. You can use a metal garbage can to store feed – it will hold about 100 pounds.
- Change all the bedding in the coop. Rake out the coop; if you can hose it out, all the better, but it's very important to make sure it's dry

before replacing the bedding. Disinfect the coop if you have a parasite problem.

- Level the chicken run floor and thoroughly clean it.
- Check the coop: Have any holes developed, any tears in the wire or anything else that requires repair?
- What season is it? Tweaks in your daily and weekly care may need to be made. If it's summer and hot and dry, there are few pests, growth of grass slows and you'll need to feed more. If there are a lot of pests and rapidly growing grass, you may need to feed your chickens less, because they will eat both the grass and pests.

Semi-Yearly Tasks

- **It's time to deep clean the coop.**
    - Remove everything you possibly can, including roosts, feeders, waterers, grit and oyster containers.
    - Sweep or use a leaf blower to get dust and other loose dirt off of walls, any light fixtures, etc.
    - *Disconnect all power to your coop!* Using a regular garden hose, rinse out the coop and soak any really nasty, soiled areas. Use your paint scraper to scrape off

the roost. You want to soften the dirt so you can easily remove it.

- Wash! Slosh the white vinegar all over the coop and scrub away! If you need to give your vinegar a bit of cleaning boost, sprinkle some baking soda and continue to scrub. If you have a high-pressure sprayer, now is the time to use it.
- Rinse well right after washing.
- Mop up any puddles and let the coop air dry
- Clean and sanitize all feeders and waterers
- When the coop is dry, put new bedding on the floor and in the nest boxes.

- **Prepare your coop for the coming season.** Add insulation if necessary, as well as heaters.
- **Worm your chickens.** Chickens get a variety of worms, including hair worm, roundworm, gizzard worm, gapeworm, and caecal worm. You can buy wormers from major pet stores or online. Get the liquid or syrup from and add it to your chicken's water per the directions.

Check if wings need clipping.

While chickens technically can't fly, they can use their wings to propel themselves over fences and walls, and even to tree branches to roost. So what's the issue?

These "flighty" birds can be a pain, but they also can put themselves in danger from traffic, local predators and irritated neighbors. While some are reluctant to cut off any part of their bird or feel it's not going to help them get away from predators, you're actually putting them in danger by leaving them unclipped–you want to be able to control their environment and keep them safe.

Check twice a year, and keep in mind that you'll have to clip their wings again after they molt, because the wing feathers will grow back.

Be sure to clip both wings; chickens will learn to adapt if you only clip one. And you're probably wondering if it hurts the chickens. Nope! It's like cutting your fingernails, and you'll be cutting through a white quill, which means it has no blood supply. Your hen won't feel a thing.

It's pretty easy to clip the wings of your chickens, but if you are hesitant to do it yourself, call your vet. Here are do-it-yourself instructions.

- **You need a pair of very sharp scissors or clippers.** If you're nervous, use clippers, or get scissors with a rounded end so you don't hurt yourself or the chicken.
- **Clip one chicken at a time.** And do not hold the chicken upside down by the legs–it's

unnecessary and cruel. People do this because the chickens will sometimes flap their wings when you're holding them. But, they're just picking up on your nervousness. Deep breaths! The calmer you are, the calmer your hen will be.

- **Have help if you can.** One person can hold the chicken while the other clips, but if that's not possible and your chicken is anxious, wrap her in a towel to calm her while she's on your knee.
- **Cut only the long flight feathers.** These are easy to find since they are the longest feathers on the chicken. There are usually 10 of these feathers.
- **Hold your hen firmly and spread out her wing.** You'll see one short feather before the long ones–after that point, clip outward toward the end of the wing, *not toward the body.*
- **Clip to just below the length of the row of shorter feathers a few inches above the flight feathers.** Do not cut into these shorter feathers.
- **If you accidentally cut feathers that have a blood supply,** don't panic. It will bleed a lot, so expect that, but grab some cornstarch, dip the wing in it and then apply pressure to the tip. If you don't have cornstarch, use a bar of soap the same way.

Collecting and Cleaning Eggs

Collecting and cleaning eggs is an important part of chicken maintenance. You don't want predators or even the chickens themselves to eat the eggs, crush them or otherwise waste your money and labor.

When to Collect Eggs

This subject was covered earlier: Eggs should be collected at least twice a day, for the reasons stated above. Now, you might have a hen that goes broody. This means that she wants to hatch eggs, and so she'll sit on them, and consume less food and water. If you want a chicken to hatch some fertilized eggs (more on this later), this is okay. But, if you want to just eat your eggs, remove the eggs from under her. If you can, move her away from the nesting area while you collect them. Broody hens can be a problem, and you'll learn more about that in chapter seven.

Chickens will lay about one unfertilized egg a day. Egg laying is stimulated by exposure to daylight. Hens reach peak laying capacity when they're exposed to 16 hours of daylight per day. If you want to maintain peak production

during the winter when the hens are in the coop, light it with a 100-watt bulb.

-University of Illinois Veterinary Teaching Hospital

If you decide to use a lamp, light it in the morning and be prepared to adjust the timing frequently to accommodate shorter and longer days.

Cleaning Eggs

Providing nice, clean bedding and nesting boxes will go a long way toward keeping your eggs clean. If the eggs are clean from the nest, don't wash them. Washing them removes the natural anti-bacterial coating on the egg, which makes it more susceptible to bacteria and spoilage.

Just give the egg shell a light rub with an abrasive cleaning pad that you use only for cleaning eggs. If another egg broke and the egg is a mess, with egg yolk and even poo all over, wash it under warm running water. Don't use cold, or the contents of the egg will shrink, a vacuum will be created, and the egg will pull in bacteria from the shell. Don't soak eggs in water, and don't use any cleaning products.

To Refrigerate or Not Refrigerate?

The subject of refrigerating eggs generates some controversy. In the United States, if eggs are commercially produced, they must be refrigerated to minimize food poisoning risk. However, in many other countries around the world, people keep eggs at room temperature for weeks with no ill effects. So how does that affect you as a backyard chicken farmer?

If in doubt, refrigerate. But, if you're feeling experimental, leave some out. Unrefrigerated eggs can be perfectly safe–it all comes down to bloom. Bloom is the natural protective layer that coats eggs, and seals the pores in eggshells to reduce the loss of moisture and prevent the development of bacteria. This bloom remains intact until the egg is washed.

If your flock is healthy, and their coop is sanitary, it's safe to leave them out. But, if you do have to wash them (this can't be repeated often enough) you must refrigerate them. If you decide to leave your eggs unrefrigerated, buy a rack that loads from the top. You want to eat the oldest eggs first.

How do you tell if an egg is still fresh enough to eat? Drop the egg in a bowl of cold water; fresh eggs will sink and eggs that are past their eat-by date will sink.

Cleaning coops and runs might not be fun, but just think of those delicious eggs and easy-to-maintain flock! You've learned about collecting eggs, how to protect them and you're armed with enough information to decide whether or not to refrigerate. Let's move on to the important topic of food and water for your birds

CHAPTER FOUR

FOOD AND WATER

Of course, food and water are essential for all life. In this chapter, you'll be reading about different types of feeds, including how to make your own, along with watering advice, and dietary supplements. As with everything else regarding chicken raising, one size does not fit all. Feeding the wrong thing can decrease egg production and also damage the health of the chickens, says The Happy Chicken Coop. Feed isn't the only thing you'll be giving your chickens, but more about that later.

Types of Feed

First, a small lesson in feed terminology:

Pellets: This is feed that is made into pellet form for easy use.

Crumbles: These are pellets that are broken into chick-size pieces to make it easy to eat.

Mash: Unprocessed chicken feed that is almost powder-like

Fermented: Any type of chicken feed mixed with water and allowed to naturally ferment.

Medicated: This feed is treated with coccidiostat to help chickens defeat any attack from coccidian protozoa, which comes from them eating food or water contaminated with infected soil or poop from infected birds. Don't use this feed if your chickens have been vaccinated.

What's in Chicken Feed?

Back in the 1900s, chickens would have to survive on table scraps and whatever they could find. Scientific research has come a long way since then, and we now know that all chicken feed should contain:

- **Protein.** The amount of protein varies based on the bird age or type of bird. For example, if you're raising a bird to eat, they will require a high protein content.
- **Amino Acids.**
- **Vitamins and Minerals.** Usually, vitamins A, E, D3 and B12 are added, as well as trace minerals like phosphorus and copper sulfate.
- **Enzymes.** These help with digestion.
- **Fiber.** This comes from the grain in the feed

- **Other additives.** You've seen commercials about Omega 3 eggs. Some feeds have Omega 3 added, which increases the amount in the eggs, making them healthier to eat.

Chickens need about 20 grams of protein a day to produce an egg.
-The Happy Chicken Coop

Be sure to read all product labels so you know what's in your feed.

When your pullets (female chickens) begin laying eggs, feed them layer feed. This feed has 16 percent protein and doesn't have as many vitamins as feed for meat chickens or chicks. If you start with one feed and change feeds, be sure to do it slowly, because a quick change can cause diarrhea or other stomach issues. This doesn't apply to the type of feed; if you start with crumbles, you can change to pellets of the same brand with no problems.

Fermented feed is healthier for your birds, and if you have a small flock, it's easy to make. In soaking the feed and grains, locked-in nutrients are released. You'll also use less feed, so it's a great way to lower your feed bill.

To make fermented feed, add water to the feed and store in a plastic or glass container with a lid (do not use metal). To make enough for three chickens, you can use a gallon-size glass jar, and fill it about one-third to one-half full with feed. Then, add bottled water (don't use tap water) to cover the grain plus two inches. Put the lid on the container and leave at room temperature for three to four days. Stir once and day and add more bottled water as needed to keep the feed covered.

The water will be cloudy and you'll see bubbles and what might appear to be a scum on the surface. This is a good thing. Just stir it all back in. Once the three-to-four days are up, if it has an unpleasant odor, toss it and start over. An alcohol smell isn't good either, but you can try to save it by adding a tablespoon of unpasteurized apple cider vinegar for each gallon of fermented feed to bring things back into balance.

Chickens love this feed. When it has a strong and sour smell (similar to yogurt) you can scoop it, strain out the liquid and feed it to them wet.

If you don't want to start over every time, this feed can act as a "starter." When you remove some, add the same amount of dry feed to the jar. Stir, put on the lid and then strain feed the next day. And, you can keep reusing the same liquid as well.

How Feed Affects Yolk Color

You'll notice that most eggs from the store or commercial farms has a sunny yellow color, and sometimes a very light yellow color. You might buy eggs from a local farmer that have a bright orange yolk. Why?

The color of the egg yolk is entirely dependent on what they're fed!

The University of Kentucky Extension says that bright orange yolks are higher in beta carotene, a type of vitamin A. You usually find these yolks in eggs from chickens that were pasture-raised on lush grass, or from legumes they've eaten.

If you want an orange yolk and can't raise your chickens on a pasture, you can add things to your chicken's diet to get an orange yolk:

- **Marigold petals**. This is what commercial chicken operations use when they want orange yolks. You can dry them and powder them and add to the feed. Or, you can buy layer feeds that have the marigold petals included.
- **Dehydrated alfalfa.**
- **Treats that are high in xanthophyll.** Xanthophyll is a plant pigment that causes the colors in fall leaves! Treats that have this pigment include carrots, apricots, pumpkin,

red cabbage, as well as the leaves of most green plants. If you spot a rooster with very yellow feet and beaks, they are probably fed this type of diet–excess pigment is stored if it's not used to make eggs.

Additions To Commercial Feeds

We'll talk about making your own chicken feed next, but there are things you can add to commercial feed to improve your flock's diet, especially if you buy a cheaper feed that doesn't supply all the dietary requirements.

If they aren't fed the correct diet, your chickens could lay fewer eggs, pick their own and other chicken's feathers, or you could get eggs that are too small or have double yolks.

Things you can add to your bird's diets include:

Black Oil Sunflower Seeds: These are cheaper than the striped kind you usually see, although they are both equally nutritious and filled with vitamin E.

Baked Crushed Eggshells: Every chicken needs calcium, and eggshells are full of it, plus they are a good replacement for chicken grit.

Dried Fruits and Vegetables: Add these just before feeding the chickens so they don't lose their taste.

Sesame Seeds: These will help your chickens feel fuller with less feed, working the same as bread in humans.

How To Make Your Own Chicken Feed

Commercial feeds are fine, but the way to fine-tune chicken egg laying and health is to make your own feed. And some people want to have first-hand knowledge of everything that goes into their chicken's food. Keep in mind that by the time you buy everything needed for complete chicken nutrition, it can cost you more than if you purchased a quality commercial feed.

There are lots of recipes online, but here are just a few:

From The Prairie Homestead:

30% Corn

30% Wheat

20% Peas

10% Oats

10% Fish Meal

2% Poultry Nutri-Balancer vitamin supplement (available online)

Kelp–source of vitamins (available online)

Aragonite Sand–for calcium (available online)

Mix everything together and feed just like commercial feed. If you prefer not to use Genetically Modified Organisms (GMO), look for non-GMO ingredients. This is a flexible recipe, as the percentage proportions mean you can make a little or a lot.

From The Homesteading Hippy, which has a recipe for laying hens:

3 parts Soft White Wheat

3 parts Hard Red Winter Wheat

1 part Hulled Barley

1 part Oat Groats

1 part Sunflower Seeds

1 part Millet

1 part Split Peas

1 part Lentils

1 part Quinoa

1 part Sesame Seeds

½ part Flax Seeds

½ part Kelp Granules

Free choice of Granite Grit

Free choice of Oyster shell

Mix everything in a container with a tight-fitting lid.

Now, you're probably asking yourself, "Where do I get all of this stuff?" You can check with your local feed store; if they don't have what you need, they should be happy to order it. You can also find all of these ingredients online.

Reducing the Cost of Feeding Chickens

You have to feed the right stuff or you're just not going to get what you want–healthy chickens that lay plenty of eggs.

Here are some tips, courtesy of Family, Food+Garden that will help you save a few dollars:

- **Raise your feeder.** A great way to save feed. Chicken's can't swish their heads and beaks to make a huge mess. Food is to eat, not play in.
- **Free Range if you can.** This may not be possible. You might not have enough land, or there are safety issues with allowing your hens to roam all over the place. But, if you

can do free-range, your chickens will scratch for bugs and nibble on plants. If you can't free-range, make your run as large as possible and add some plants.

- **Grow a Chicken Garden.** This is a great idea if you free-range or can just build a large run. Plant things like lettuce, buckwheat, cabbage, beets, kale, spinach, purslane and comfrey. You can also plant amaranth, which grow seed heads with seeds chickens love.
- **Kitchen and garden scraps.** As you'll read in the last chapter, Chicken Stories, having a family and lots of food waste can provide free chicken feed.

But before you run off to buy plants for your chickens, make sure that you're getting those that are safe for chickens, per 104homestead.com:

Flowering Plants: Bee Balm, Begonia, Black Eyed Susan, Coreopsis, Calendula, Daisy, Dandelion, Day Lily, Echinacea, Impatiens, Marigold, Nasturtium, Orchid, Petunia, Sunflower, Thistle, Velvet Nettle, Violet, Zinnia.

Foliage Plants: Coleus, Hens & Chicks, Hosts, Yucca.

Herbs: Catnip, Lavender, Lemon Balm, Mint, Oregano, Rosemary.

Vines: Black Eyed Susan, Bougainvillea, Grape Ivy, Nasturtium, Rose, Swedish ivy, Virginia Creeper,

Shrubs: Bamboo, Butterfly Bush, Dogwood, Fig, Gardenia, Hop Tree, Juniper, Lilac, Palm, Rose.

Trees: Citrus, Crab Apple, Dogwood, Elm, Eucalyptus, Fig, Guava, Hawthorn, Hop Tree, Madrona, Magnolia, Manzanita, Palm, Papaya, Pine, Redbud, Sassafras, Willow.

If you already have things planted near where you want to locate your coop, these plants, Cornell University Department of Agriculture and Life Sciences has an extensive list of plants that are poisonous for livestock:

http://poisonousplants.ansci.cornell.edu/php/plants.php?action=list with both scientific and common names. Check it out. Better safe than sorry!

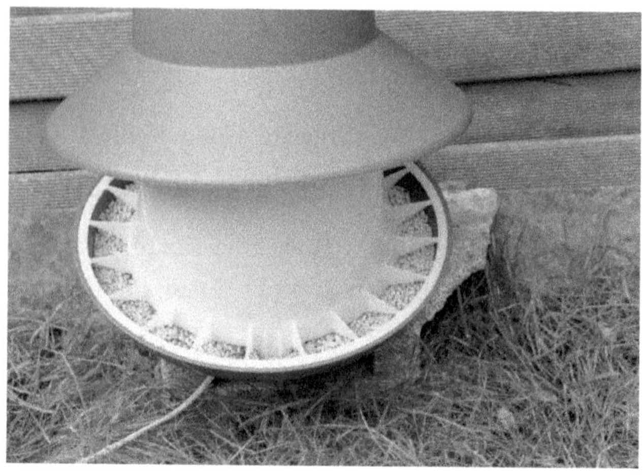

Chicken Snacks

Just like people, chickens love snacks, and they can provide a nutritional boost as well. As The Happy Chicken Coop says, they add variety to their diet, and snacks make chickens happy! Just keep in mind that you can spend a lot of money on chicken treats – in fact, 75 percent of the cost of keeping chickens is for food. This list of treats gives some affordable options:

Oatmeal: A great treat when it's cold outside. Just make some extra when you make your own breakfast. You can pour it straight into their feeding trough; if you just put a pan down, they can bully each other since they can't all get to it at once. You can add fruit or even maple syrup to give them some variety.

Cottage Cheese: You can feed this straight out of the tub or mix in some vegetables. It provides calcium, and it's a great source of protein.

Pasta and Noodles: Picture this: Your favorite chicken running around with pasta streaming from their beak. Adorable! Cooked pasta is cheap and filling, and two cups of it is more than enough for six chickens. You can mix in other foods or use a creamy sauce, but they will be happy with just the plain cooked noodles.

Mealworms: They're not just for fishing! Chickens love, love, love mealworms. Buy a one pound bag of them and dump them in a pile in the chicken run. You can buy these from your local bait store, but they can be expensive, so if you plan to give them to your chickens on a regular basis, you might want to farm your own mealworms -- Bugible.com tells you how. If DIY isn't your thing, you can buy kits online. Be warned, however, that some people eat mealworms, so if you don't fancy eating worms, you might want to not view some kits right after eating!

How To Farm Your Own Mealworms:

Step 1: Find a location. Mealworms like the dark, and at the minimum low light. They also like a temperature around 80 degrees Fahrenheit. If you don't have a spot that's warm enough, you can buy a heat mat, made for reptiles for less than $20. The ideal temperature is between 77 degrees and 81 degrees. Mealworm growth is negatively impacted by temperatures below 62 degrees and above 86 degrees.

Step 2: The Container. The recommended size is 12 inches x 24 inches x 12 inches deep. A plastic storage tote works well. Or, if you are handy, you can build a multi-tiered mealworm farm; plans are available online. A multi-tiered solution might be idea because adult worms can eat the pupae or eggs. Make sure your container is clean and dry, and make sure you either use screening for the top or poke holes in the lid for ventilation.

Step 3: Add the Feed. There are a number of things you can use to feed your mealworms, including wheat bran, rolled oats, chicken mash or cereal crumbs. Make sure, if you use chicken feed, that it doesn't contain diatomaceous earth, because this will kill your mealworms.

Your worms will get most of their moisture from vegetable scraps. Add peels and rinds from fruits and vegetables, but don't add fruits that will rot fast and make the worm habitat moist. Mold is something you want to avoid.

Step 4: Buy Mealworms. Buy mealworms online or at a pet store or online. Plan to order around 500.

Step 5: Add the Worms to Your Container. Pour (gently, now) your mealworms into the container and put on the cover. Remember, use mesh or screen or make sure the lid has holes.

Step 6: Feed Your Worms. Keep them fed and watch them multiply! You can feed them as much as you want; feeding more means more worms. At the least, feed them at least every few weeks and maintain around three inches of depth.

Step 7: Time to Harvest! Keep in mind that mealworms are not really worms at all. They are the larvae of the mealworm beetle, which is a species of darkling beetle. It takes five to six months for the worms to turn into beetles. So, harvest your worms after three months. If you have pupae and beetles, leave them in your farm so they can reproduce. And, the larvae will eat the dead beetles. There's not much cleaning involved with mealworms; just remove any moldy food.

And easy trick to collect the worms is to add new feed. A carrot works well. Put it in the container and leave it for a few minutes. The worms will latch onto the carrot, so you can pull it out and shake it over a separate container to collect your wormy chicken snacks.

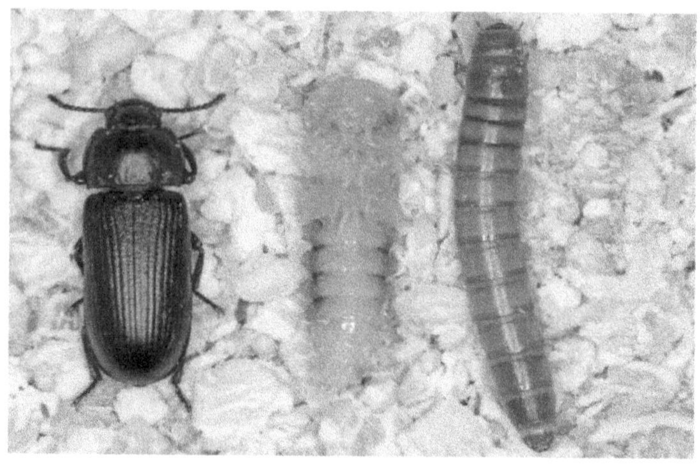

The beatle, pupae and larva (worm) stage of the darkling beetle

What to Expect:

- During the 2-to-three-month lifespan of the darkling beetle, a female can lay up to thousands of eggs.
- Eggs take an average of 12 days to hatch.
- They hatch as a tiny, white larva that's difficult to see.
- Larva will go through up to 20 molts, shedding its exoskeleton as it grows. Their last molt is when they're about three months old. It will then be golden brown and a bit over an inch long..

- This is when you harvest your mealworms. If not, it will pupate, and then in six to 18 days, you'll get beetles.

That's everything you wanted (or didn't want!) to know about mealworms. If they aren't something you want to deal with, there are plenty of other tasty treats!

Corn: You can give your chickens sweetcorn loose or mix with their food. Or, you can give it straight from the cob. Just buy some ears, and hang them up using string. The hens will peck away for hours! This is a cheap treat, and it's full of phytochemicals to keep your flock's eyes healthy, and corn has lots of fiber.

Watermelon: It's full water and essential vitamins and minerals. In hot weather, it's a refreshing treat. You can cut the watermelon into small chunks, freeze them, and then put them in the water dishes.

Pumpkin: The seeds in pumpkins help your chickens get rid of tapeworms. Just put the pumpkin in the run and hit it with a mallet to break it open. Not only is this a healthy, tasty snack, you'll enjoy bright orange yolks for a few days.

Scrambled Eggs: If you find yourself with too many eggs, you can cook them up for your hens. They are full of protein and filling. Do not ever feed your chickens raw eggs – they will start eating their own.

Want your hens to lay more eggs? Mealworms, scrambled eggs, greens and fruit can all help.

How To Feed Your Chickens

Old movies set on farms usually show someone tossing feed on the ground for chickens. What a waste! It's equally important not to have feeders on the round in the run or on the floor of the coop; the chickens will toss it all over and maybe even poop in it.

There are many types of feeders, and you can keep them outside in the run, or in your coop, if it is large enough. Keep in mind that when your chickens roost at night, they sleep and won't get up to eat or drink. But, it's all-too-easy for predators to get to food when it's left outside.

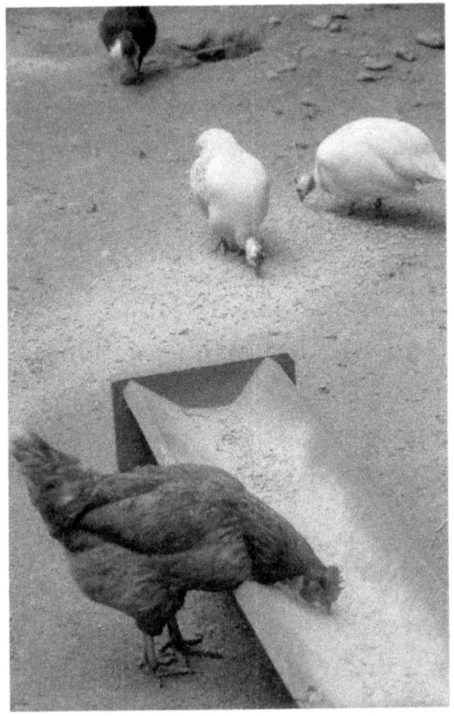

Metal or Plastic? Metal feeders are harder to find, but they often outlast plastic feeders; sun and snow are hard on plastic.

Automatic/Treadle Feeders: This is a great option if you have to work late or travel. The hens have to learn to stand on the platform in order for the feed box to open. Chickens are smart. They'll learn fast. But, raccoons are smart, too, so if you have a feeder like this and leave it outside, be sure you have a way to lock it.

Hanging Feeders: These are also known as "gravity feeders," because that's how they work. It's a large bucket with a ring underneath that holds the food. Per The Happy Chicken Coop, these are hands-down the best selling type of feeder, whether they hang, or are mounted on a wall or in a corner. Have a couple of these in your coop so the chickens don't all crowd at once. And, there are some bully hens who will guard a feeder as her property, which means no one else gets to eat. So, have more than one. If you plan to feed outside, some come with rain guards to prevent food from getting wet.

Trough Feeders: This type of feeder is especially popular for small chicks, but one of the best things about this style is that many hens can fit around the feeder at the same time. Make sure if you buy this type of feeder that it comes with legs to keep it above the ground. And, an advantage of this feeder is that chickens don't sit in it, so they can't poop in it. Also be sure to get a modern tube-and-trough gravity feeder to keep the feed from getting dirty.

Pest Proof: Look for this kind of feeder if you're having a problem with things like rats or mice.

Chick Feeders: You'll learn more about raising chicks later, but these are smaller versions adult feeders. Many of them have round bases so you can fill a Mason jar with feed and screw it into the base.

Dietary Supplements

If you buy a good, age-appropriate, nutritionally-balanced chicken feed, your flock will have what they need for basic health. But, there are supplements you can give your chickens to give them a health boost.

Chickens can also need things like vitamins if they are under stress, during very cold weather, when they're breeding, or if they're ill. Chicks can get off to a good start with multivitamins in their water.

Grit: Chickens that aren't free range or don't have access to dirt and gravel need grit. When in the wild, chickens pick up small pieces of gravel and store it in their gizzard. The gravel acs like teeth and helps break up the chicken's food. You can feed your chickens grit in a separate container from their food.

Calcium: Of course, calcium is essential for proper shell formation. Most feeds for laying hens have calcium added, but if a hen isn't getting enough of it, she'll pull calcium from her bones to produce eggshells. Supplement calcium if you notice soft egg shells–they will be rubbery instead of hard. You can do this by offering either crushed eggshells or you can buy an oyster shell supplement from your local feed store or online.

Apple Cider Vinegar: Apple cider vinegar can thin mucus if your chickens have respiratory issues, it helps with digestion, and it can help get rid of parasites by providing an alkaline environment. But be sure to buy apple cider vinegar that has the "mother" intact. This is the live bacteria in the vinegar that gives all the health benefits. Look for unfiltered apple cider vinegar, as it's more likely to still have the "mother." Add a tablespoon per gallon of fresh water, and rotate with plain water every other day.

Electrolytes: If your flock is feeling stressed, electrolytes are the perfect addition. Chickens can get stress from being transported, additions to the flock, extreme heat or illness. You can buy packaged electrolytes in most feed stores or online. Read the package directions on how much to add to the flock's water.

Probiotics: Probiotics aid your chicken's digestive health and their immune system. Sprinkle probiotics over their food or add to the bird's drinking water. You can buy probiotic powders at most feed stores and online. As with everything else, follow the package directions.

Garlic: Chickens eggs reflect what your chickens eat, but don't worry about garlic-flavored eggs! Garlic is wonderful for fighting respiratory issues in your chickens. Chop fresh garlic and add it to their feed or use powdered garlic; one tablespoon per gallon of feed.

Diatomaceous earth: Add boxes of sand mixed with diatomaceous earth to your chicken run for your hens to "bathe" in. Chickens bathe in dust, and adding diatomaceous earth can help kill parasites like lice and mites. Be sure to always buy food quality diatomaceous earth. If you don't want to make boxes, just sprinkle it in an area where your chickens already roll.

Diatomaceous earth is the crushed shells of diatoms, which are fossilized aquatic algae. It's composed mostly of silica, clay minerals iron oxide. It kills soft-body insects by causing them to dry out.

A study performed by the University of California at Riverside showed that chickens that rolled in a dust bath of sand mixed with diatomaceous earth had a huge reduction in external parasites in just a week. Some feed their chickens diatomaceous earth, but research has shown mixed results when it comes to its effectiveness in eliminating internal parasites.

Molasses: Blackstrap molasses is high in iron, magnesium, potassium and calcium It also can be used as a laxative. In small amounts, it can help a hen recover from an illness or shock. Add 16 ounces per five gallons of water.

Protein: You'll want to add protein when your chickens are molting. Molting is when your chickens shed feathers to make room for new growth. You'll read more about molting in chapter six. Healthy sources of protein include eggs, cooked poultry, meat scraps and bones, fish, shellfish, mealworms, nuts and seeds, oats, sprouts and chick feed. If you use chick feed, don't substitute completely, but use as a snack or mix it with their regular feed.

The Importance Of Consistent Watering

It's hard to overemphasize the importance of water for chickens. The website Abundant Permaculture states that:

Just a few hours without access to water can critically affect egg production and

24 hours without water can cause a loss of eggs for 24 days.

Ouch! If that doesn't convince you to keep your chickens watered, nothing will. Here are some tips for keeping your flock well watered:

- In your run, keep the waterers clean; scrub them daily. Keep the water on a platform or block so the chickens don't scratch debris or poop in it.
- Four adult chickens will drink about a quart of water a day, and up to twice that much if it's hot.
- Make sure there's water always available.
- Make sure the water is clean, clean, clean.
- You don't have to keep water out all night because chickens will settle on a perch and

won't get down until the morning, so in winter, move the water to a warm place in your home overnight so it doesn't freeze.

Water, water everywhere. But what do you put it in? What are the best waterers? The folks at Backyard Poultry have some suggestions.

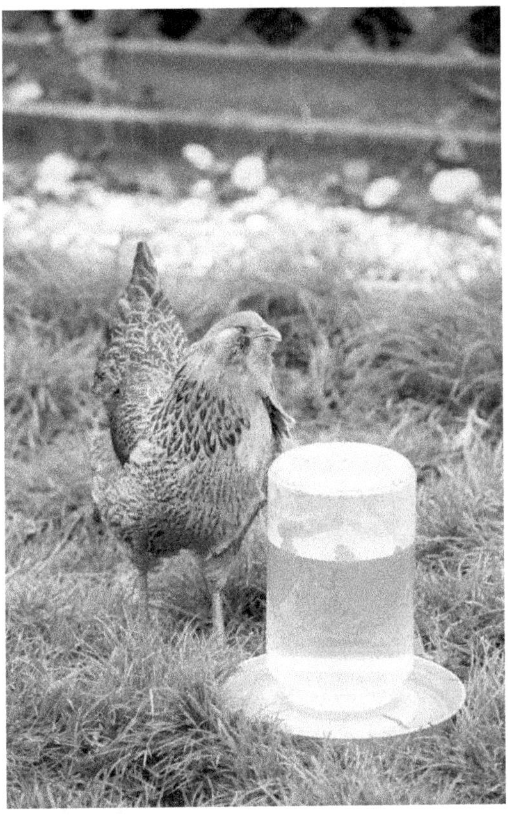

Chicken with Gravity-Style Chicken Waterer

The Correct Waterer For your Chicken's Size And Age

In the next chapter, you'll read about laying hens and raising chicks. This section of chapter four will discuss different watering options for chickens of different sizes and ages. After all, you might not only have baby chicks, but you might have bantams as well as full-size hens.

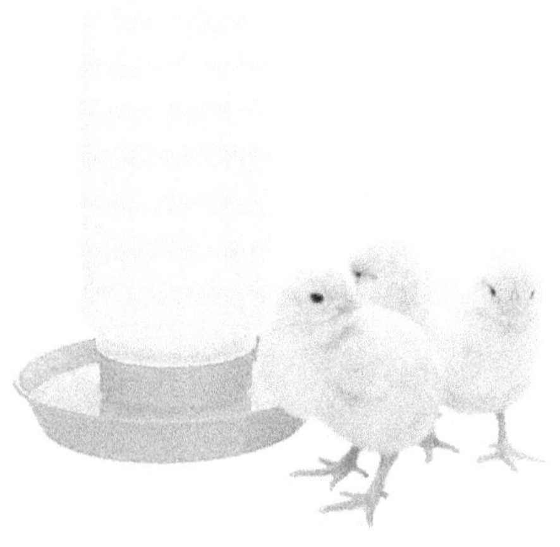

Baby chicks need access to water at all times. But, never give them water in an open dish or bowl. They will talk into it and poop, get wet and chilled, or even drown. Start with a one-quart waterer. You can buy a screw-on base that fits a narrow-mouth jar, or buy a special waterer. There's also something called a drown-proof waterer. All of these things are very inexpensive. A one-quart waterer will give 25 chicks in a brooder enough water for the first few days after they hatch.

In those first few days, put the water on a flat surface that's sturdy; like a square of plywood or a large tile. This will steady the base so it won't tip and leak, and it helps keep brooder litter out of the water.

In a week or two, your chicks will outgrow their waterer, and it's time to move to a one-gallon waterer. But, leave the old waterer there until the chicks get used to it. You know you need a larger capacity waterer if you have to keep refilling the one-quart or if the chicks have gotten so big that they knocked over their waterer while playing.

For adults, pullets and chicks, there are all-in-one solutions. The key is to adapt the height of the waterer to accommodate chicks and pullets.

There are basically two types of chicken waterers:

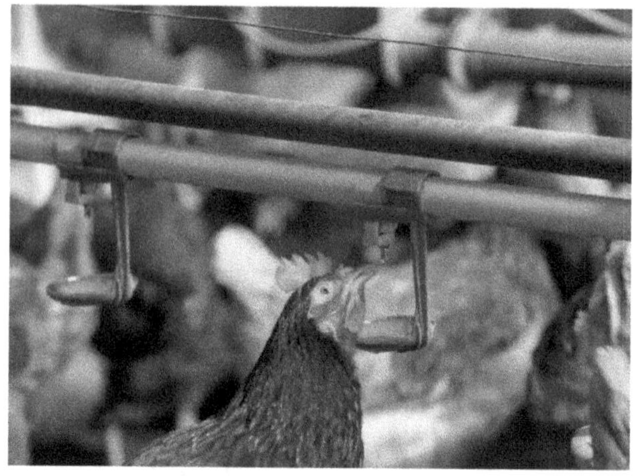

Automatic Chicken Waterer with cups

Gravity Style Chicken Waterer: This type of chicken waterer has a plastic or metal tank that can be filled from the top or bottom, and water flows into a circular dish or tray. Keep in mind that though the water in the tank stays clean, the dish gets dirty easily.

Automatic Chicken Waterer: This type of waterer is very hygienic and gives chickens the freshest water. They come with cups, as in the photo, or with nipples. This type of waterer is a great choice if you need to save space in your chicken coop. This type of waterer generally needs to be assembled.

Keeping Your Chickens Watered

But what size waterer? Chicken waterer tanks come in one gallon, two-and-a-half-gallon, five gallon or eight gallon. The smaller tanks work well for a brood of four chickens. You'll want the larger size if you have more than four chickens.

Chickens can be finicky, and if you're having problems getting your chickens to drink from an automatic waterer, there are videos online that will show you how to train your chickens to use it. A small amount of dripping water will also encourage them to drink.

Place your tank where it won't get knocked over. And nipples and cups can leak, so if you have to seal them, use a waterproof sealant.

You've read about coops, what chickens to buy, how to feed and water them. Let's look a little deeper at laying hens, collecting and cleaning eggs, incubating eggs and raising chicks.

CHAPTER FIVE

LAYING HENS, EGGS AND CHICKS

Unless you have a rooster, your hens will lay unfertilized eggs. However, you can buy fertilized eggs from a hatchery, either locally or online. You can even buy them on popular auction sites and even on Amazon.com! That being said, sites like Raising Happy Chickens recommend you buy from a local, independent breeder so you know what you're getting.

So, what else should you know before deciding to hatch eggs?

Buying Fertilized Eggs

- If you buy online, make sure whoever is selling them packages them well and marks them fragile.
- Fertilized eggs that have traveled, whether by common carrier or in your car, have to be stored safely and rest for at least 12

hours before putting them in an incubator **with the pointed end facing downward.**

- Keep the eggs cool and moist, but not cold. This means you don't put them in the refrigerator.
- Eggs should be put in the incubator seven days or less after they've been laid. After that, fertility begins to fall and you'll get lower hatch rates.
- Then, check the eggs by candling. Although it's called "candling," you won't really be using a candle. Instructions for candling an egg, per the University of Lincoln:
    - Use a bright light. You can use a really bright flashlight. An LED flashlight would be ideal, since it doesn't get hot.
    - Candle in a dark room, either near the incubator or in the same room as the incubator. You'll need to put the eggs right back in when you're done.
    - Don't be nervous, but if you are, practice on a grocery store egg.
    - Hold the large end of the egg up to the light and slowly turn it until you

can see the inside of the egg. You should see the pores in the shell, the yolk, blood vessels, and an embryo, and if the egg's been in the incubator for a week, you might even see the embryo move.

- Toss out any eggs with cracks. You can't fix them, and they probably won't hatch. And, you don't want any bacteria in the crack to contaminate the incubator.
- If the shell is porous, it will look mottled when candled. Some mottling is fine, but if there's too much, the egg probably won't hatch.

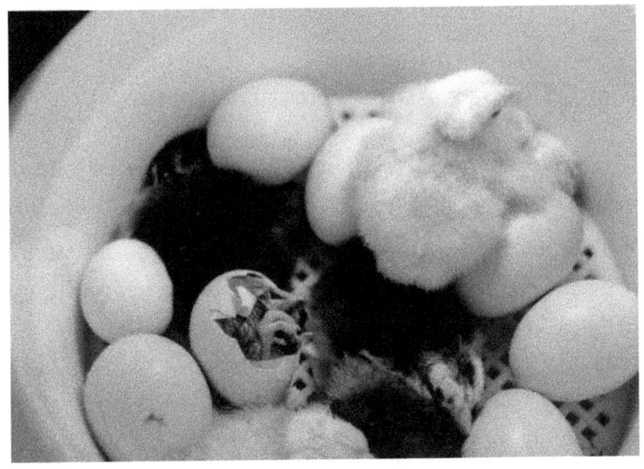

Incubating Eggs – You Can't Trust The Hen

You have your fertilized eggs and you've let them settle for 12 hours or more in a cool, moist environment. Now, how will you hatch them?

You really can't trust the hen. The Modern Farmer says modern hens aren't really the best mothers. They aren't sure if it's genetic or cultural; they get distracted, other hens push them out of their nest or a good-looking rooster comes by… All sorts of things can go wrong.

Of course, you can just buy chicks, but what's the fun in that? Most farmers and backyard chicken fans do the brood work themselves.

It takes 21 days on average for an egg to hatch once incubation begins.

-Modern Farmer
Choosing the Perfect Incubator

You can spend $50 for an incubator or you can spend thousands. Or, you can build your own from instructions on the web. You can find instructions from everything from a styrofoam box with a wire rack and a light bulb to a fancy cabinet incubator.

No matter if it's DIY or store-bought, an incubator has to control:

Temperature: The fertilized eggs must be kept at 99.5 degrees at all times. Even one degree higher or lower can terminate the embryo after a few hours.

Humidity: For the first 18 days, you must maintain 40 percent to 50 percent humidity. After that, keep the humidity at 65 percent to 75 percent.

Ventilation: You've read about how eggshells are porous. This lets oxygen enter, and carbon dioxide to exit, so incubators have to have holes or vents to allow fresh air to circulate.

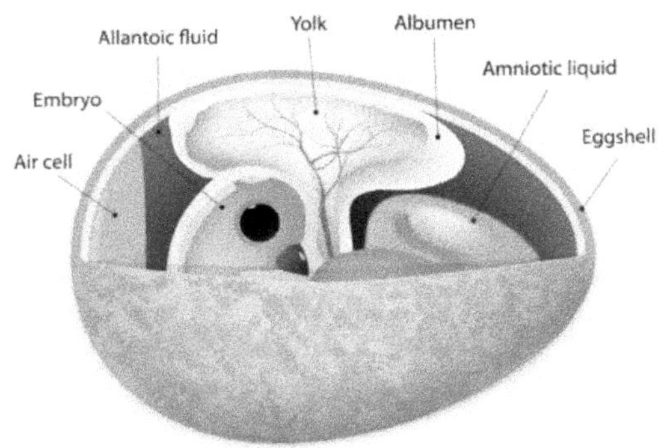

The Incubating Process: What To Do When

One of the most important tools of incubation is a high-quality thermometer and hygrometer (a hygrometer measures humidity). This is one thing to splurge on–cheap models aren't very accurate, and you don't want to lose your chickens because you didn't want to spend the money. Buy a combo thermometer/hygrometer with an external display; the sensor goes into the incubator and you can read the instrument without having to open the incubator. You wouldn't want to ruin your carefully-calibrated hatching chamber.

Before you place the eggs inside the incubator, turn on the heat and measure the temperature and humidity over 24 hours, and make adjustments as necessary.

Some incubators will turn the eggs automatically, but if you're going to turn the eggs yourself:

- Draw an "X" on one side of the egg and an "O" on the other so you know which eggs have been turned.
- Three times a day or more, gently turn the eggs over. The more often you turn the eggs the better, but make sure it's an odd number so they are never resting on the same side for two nights in a row. Some experts recommend alternating the direction of the turning each time to vary the embryo position as much as possible.
- Keep turning the eggs until day 18, and then leave them alone until they hatch.
- Before you place the eggs inside the incubator, turn on the heat and measure the temperature and humidity over 24 hours, and make adjustments as necessary.

You might see the eggs shifting around on their own as the fetus becomes active in the final days before hatching. The chick will take its first breath after pecking a small hole in the large end of the egg. The chick will rest for six to 12 hours as it's lungs adjust before it continues to hatch.

Do not assist in the hatching process–it's too easy to cause injury to the fragile chick.

After your chick is free of the egg, let it dry off in the incubator before moving it to your brooder; that's where your chicks will spend the first weeks of its life.

Raising Chicks

You now have baby chicks! As mentioned in the section on hatching chicks, your chicks will spend their first few weeks in a brooder. Again, you can buy a brooder or find a plan on the web and do it yourself.

The size will depend on the number of chicks; you should have a minimum of two-and-a-half square feet per chick. More is definitely better, says Backyard Chickens.

On the bottom of the brooder, put a layer of clean litter–pine shavings are ideal–and do not use newspaper or any kind of paper. It's too slippery and can cause leg and foot problems for the chicks. For very small chicks, put some paper towels over the shavings to stop them pecking and eating the shavings until they figure out what food is! Change this litter every couple of days. Cleanliness is VERY important now. Never allow the litter to get damp. Baby chicks easily get a number of diseases that thrive in a damp environment (more about chicken diseases in chapter six).

Add a low roost about four inches from the floor when the chicks are about a month old. This will encourage them to start roosting. Make sure not to put it right under the heat lamp because it will be too warm.

The brooder temperature should be around 90 degrees fahrenheit in the warmest part of the brooder for the first week. After that, lower the temperature around five degrees every week until the chicks have their adult feathers, at about five-to-eight-weeks old. Provide warmer and cooler areas in the brooder so the baby chicks can regulate their comfort level.

Watch the chicks–if they are panting or huddling in corners furthest from the light, they're too hot. If they're in a ball under the light, they're too cold. You can either change the wattage of the bulb or increase or decrease the distance from the chicks. DO NOT USE TEFLON COATED BULBS. The gas coming off of them can quickly kill your chicks.

Food and Water

As you've already learned, fresh, clean water is incredibly important. Put your waterer as far as possible from the heat lamp. If you're using a bowl for water, fill it with marbles or clean pebbles so the chicks don't drown or get soaked if they fall it. Chicks are very clumsy!

Chicks, like adult chickens, will scratch at their food, so a feeder that keeps the food as much as possible in one place is good. Cleanliness here is very important because the chicks will poop into their own food, so you'll often be cleaning the feeder and refilling it.

Start your chicks out with crumbles (see chapter four) or "chick starter." This is specially formulated, age appropriate food that meets the chick's dietary requirements. You can buy non-medicated feed or feed that's been medicated with a small amount of drugs that helps prevent Coccidiosis (covered in the next chapter). But, again, cleanliness is important–medicated food doesn't provide 100 percent protection.

Your chick crumbles are a complete food, but after the first week or two, you can give your baby chicks small amounts of treats daily. It's important when feeding treats to offer them grit in separate bowls to help break down the new food. Look for chick-size grit, but if you can't find it, coarse sand works. Good treats for baby chicks include things like a mashed up hard boiled egg, chopped strawberries and other fruit, mealworms, grapes, and even crickets. View treats the same way as candy for kids–give it to your chicks sparingly.

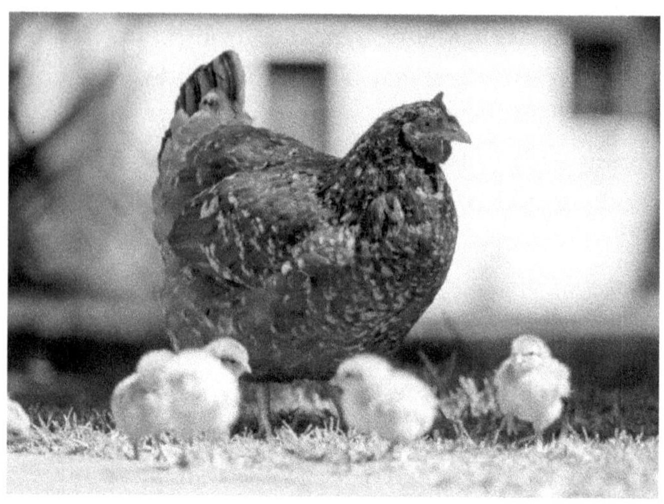

Other Requirements

Chicks are incredibly curious, and after the first week or two, they can go outside for short periods if the temperature is high enough. But they must be watched at this age. They can move fast, can squeeze into small spaces, and they are completely helpless against predators. Make sure they're in a secure enclosure.

If chicks have bonded to you, they will probably follow you around. They become fond of their owners, and some will even come when you call them.

Keep their outdoor time short while the chicks get used to the idea, and then gradually increase the time as they grow up. Not only is this play time for the chicks, but it will make the eventual transition to a coop easier for both of you.

Unfortunately, baby chicks often get something called "pasty butt." This is when their droppings stick to their vent (located under the chicken's tail) and clog it, making it impossible for them to poop or pee. Especially during the first two weeks, check the chick's bottoms every few hours. If you find a pasty bottom, soak and remove the plug carefully, pat the area dry and apply a little vaseline or vegetable oil. Note that apple cider vinegar can help prevent pasty butt–use three-to-four-tablespoons per gallon of water.

You have your chickens, you've incubated eggs and you're raising chicks. How do you keep everyone healthy, hearty and laying as many eggs as possible? Read on!

CHAPTER SIX

HEALTHY CHICKENS ARE HAPPY CHICKENS

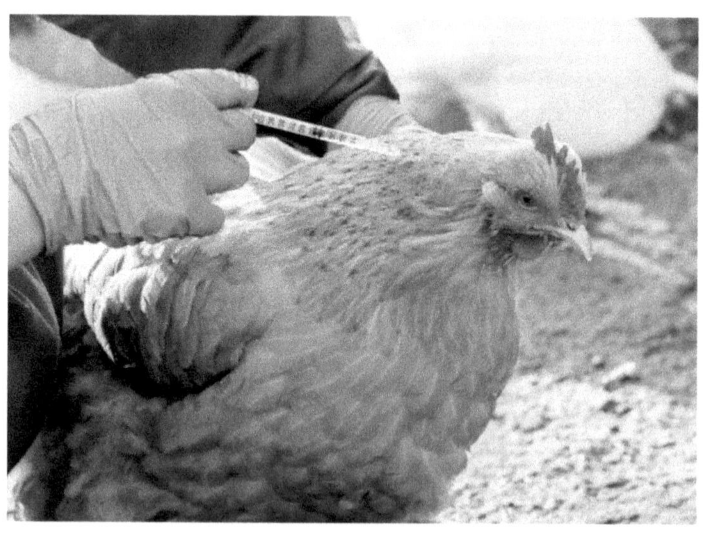

Of course you want to keep your chickens healthy. The first important thing is to find a poultry vet; ask around or consult poultrydvm.com to find one in your area. This chapter will explore common illnesses, common pests and traditional and alternative methods of healthcare.

You can't control everything when it comes to raising chickens. You can guard against predators, but things still happen. Pests are a fact of life. You can't prevent all diseases. And you can't always keep your chickens from injuring themselves or others in the flock.

Chicken-raising experts all agree that biosecurity is an important preventative tool for healthy chickens. These are things you do every day, like keeping your coop, nesting boxes, perch, run, waterers and feeders clean. But, there are other important measures that you can take:

- **Different age chickens shouldn't mix.** Younger, smaller birds can be seen as intruders and bullied as other hens work to establish a pecking order. Or, the other chickens may try to drive them away, and in extreme cases, kill them. The exception is if one of the hens of the current flock hatches eggs. It's entirely normal for a hen to go off by herself to incubate her eggs and then return to the flock with her chicks; she'll be accepted.
- **Clean and disinfect supplies after each use.** This isn't the usual disinfecting. This applies to

transport coops and their feeders and waterers. Remember, bacteria can linger for months.

- **Keep your hens at home.** Your flock can pick up all kinds of stuff if you let them wander off of your property or take them to events where they can mix with other birds, like swap meets or chicken shows, and then bring them back.
- **Quarantine:** You don't want sick birds infecting your flock, so keep any new chickens you get a minimum of 30 feet from the rest of your birds for 30 days. Make sure the new birds are in perfect health before introducing them to the rest of your chickens.
- **No mingling.** Birds share germs, mites and intestinal parasites, so keep your chickens away from other types of poultry (ducks, geese, turkeys), and pet and wild birds.
- **Disinfect any shared equipment.** If you happen to share or borrow any equipment with a fellow chicken fan, disinfect it before you bring it in contact with your flock.
- **Limit visitors.** You'll probably want to invite friends over to see your beautiful coop and friendly chickens. Just make sure they wash their hands and that their shoes are clean; you don't want them bringing any bacteria or pests into your flock's domain.

Your Chicken First Aid Kit

Your philosophy of chicken raising will determine what you have in your first aid kit. Later, you'll read about traditional healthcare as well as alternative methods. The Dummies book of hobby farming advises that at minimum, you should have a hospital cage to isolate and assess chickens that are injured or sick, plus have the means to humanely euthanize a bird that is hopelessly sick.

Other items you might want to have in your first aid kit include:

- A heat lamp and bulb to warm a chilled chicken; get the kind you can hang securely, and keep away from the clamp-style.
- A mister, electric fan or other device to cool a hot chicken.
- Antiseptic solution and 10ml syringe for flushing wounds. Use hydrogen peroxide, iodine or Betadine. This is for shallow wounds only. For deep wounds, or if the wound gets infected, please call your vet.
- A pair of tweezers for looking at wounds and removing debris.
- A pair of scissors to remove bandages.
- Gauze sponges for cleaning wounds and blotting them.
- Styptic pencil, styptic powder or cornstarch to stop bleeding.

- Rolls of adhesive cloth bandages for dressing feet or wings. Buy one-inch and two-inch.
- Vitamin and electrolyte supplements that you can mix with drinking water.
- Water-based personal lubricant to help a prolapsed vent or egg-bound bird.
- Your vet's phone number. Also be sure to have this programed into your mobile phone!

Common Diseases

In a backyard flock, serious diseases aren't very likely, especially if you vaccinate your chickens (more about this later in the chapter), but it's good to know the signs and symptoms of these diseases, because your chickens can get them from wild birds and other sources. Also, some chicken aficionados don't like to vaccinate. Here are the most common diseases that can affect your flock. Information for this section came from Mississippi State University Extension and the Morning Chores website.

- **Fowl Cholera**. There is a vaccine for this illness. But, sometimes vaccines are ineffective, or maybe your choose not to vaccinate. Watch for: Greenish or yellowish diarrhea, joint pain, and a darkened head or wattle. It's spread by infected birds, but not through the egg. It can be transmitted to raccoons, possums, dogs, cats, pigs and vermin.

There is no treatment for this disease, and if your bird does survive, she'll always be a carrier. Humane euthanization and destruction of the carcass is really your only option if you don't want to infect the entire flock.

- **Botulism**. You can avoid botulism if you keep your chickens in an environment that's clean and free from any dead carcass. Botulism is a serious disease caused by dead meat near their food and water, with resulting contamination. If infected, your chicken(s) will have progressing tremors; if left untreated, the tremors progress and causes total body paralysis. Death usually occurs within a few hours.

  Your local vet can provide an antitoxin, but it can be expensive. If you catch the disease early enough, you can treat your chicken by giving them a daily dropper of one teaspoon Epsom salts mixed with warm water.

- **Infectious Bronchitis.** If you hear your chickens sneezing, snoring and coughing, it could be infectious bronchitis. They'll start having drainage from their nose and eyes. They will also stop laying.

There is a vaccine for infectious bronchitis, but if you decide not to vaccinate, you'll have to move quickly when you see the signs–it's a viral disease that will travel through the air and quickly infect your flock.

Give infected chickens a warm, dry place to recover. Some give their birds a warm herbal tea and fresh herbs to aid their healing.

- **Infectious Coryza.** Infectious Coryza usually happens in semi-mature and adult birds. It can either manifest as a slow-spreading chronic disease that only affects a small number of birds, or as a rapidly-spreading disease with a larger number of affected birds. It's not a widespread disease, fortunately. When infected, the chicken's head becomes swollen, including the combs and their eyes swell shut. Discharge will flow from the bird's eyes and nose, they'll have moisture under their wings and they will stop laying.

  There is no vaccine for this disease, nor is there any treatment. Your only option is to humanely euthanize and destroy the carcass to keep other birds from being infected. This disease is spread from contaminated water and birds. Again, cleanliness is a top priority for disease prevention.

- **Mareks' Disease.** Marek's Disease (named after a Hungarian veterinarian) is usually a disease found in young birds. It's concentrated in the feather follicles. It's shed through dander (dead skin and feather cells) where it has a long survival time. Symptoms of this disease include tumor growth inside or outside your chicks. Also their iris will turn gray and they won't respond to light. Paralysis follows. This disease is very easy for your birds to catch, since it's transmitted through the air by the chicks breathing in the dander.

  There is a vaccine for Marek's Disease, usually given to day-old chicks. If your chick(s) get this disease, there is no alternative but humane euthanization.

- **Thrush.** Thrush in chickens is similar to thrush that infects human babies. Chickens infected with thrush have a white, oozy discharge inside their crop (the space between their neck and body), a larger-than-normal appetite, and a crusty vent. Their feathers will look rumpled and will be lethargic.

  Thrush is treated with antifungal medication from your vet. There is no vaccine. This is a fungal disease, which means your chickens can get it from eating moldy feed or food or from contaminated water. Remove any bad food and clean their feeder and waterer.

- **Air Sac Disease.** Air sac disease first manifests in chickens as weakness and a lack of laying. You'll then see sneezing, breathing problems, coughing, swollen joints and even death.

  There is a vaccine for this disease, and it can be treated by your vet with antibiotics, but it can be transferred from a hen to her fertilized chick. Stay alert for any of these symptoms and contact your vet right away.

- **Mushy Chick.** Its name says it - Mushy Chick affects newly hatched chicks. They will have an enlarged, blue-tinted, inflamed midsection. The chick will appear drowsy and have an unpleasant smell; it will also be week. It's scientific name is Colibacillosis, and it's caused by E.Coli bacteria.

  Warning: Use caution when handling chicks with this disease. Make sure you have no open wounds on your hands or wear latex gloves. Staph and strep bacteria are in this disease, and these can infect humans.

  There's no vaccine for Mushy Chick. It's transmitted from chick-to-chick or by a dirty surface where an infected chick has been, or an unclean area where a chick gets the disease because of a weak immune system. Sometimes, antibiotics will work for this disease, but no matter what, quarantine the sick chicks.

- **Pullorum.** Pullorum disease is either an acute (fast acting) or chronic (ongoing) infectious disease. In chicks, symptoms include lack of activity, white paste on their butts, and have problems breathing. But some will die with no symptoms at all. In adult birds, you'll see them sneezing and coughing and not laying.

  There's no vaccine for this disease. It's primarily egg transmitted, but it can also come from an infected hen to egg, egg to chick, incubating-chick-to-incubating-chick, contaminated areas or from contaminated clothes, shoes or equipment. Because it's a viral disease, there's no treatment but humane euthanization and destruction of the carcass.

- **Avian Influenza.** When you hear about "bird flu," they're talking about avian influenza. What you'll hear on the news is that people are getting sick from chickens, but what you might not know that, according to the United States Department of Agriculture, only 10 percent of infected chickens came from backyard flocks and 90 percent of infected chickens are from commercial operations.

Healthy chickens sometimes show no symptoms, but watch for the following, and act quickly: Respiratory problems, diarrhea, face swelling, and a discolored or blue wattle and comb. Your hens will stop laying, and they make have dark red spots on their legs and combs.

There is no vaccine, and wild animals can carry the disease from bird-to-bird. Infected chickens, if they survive, will always be carriers. The only real solution is human euthanization and destruction of the carcass. Use caution, a face mask and rubber gloves, because, again, this disease can be spread to humans.

- **Bumblefoot.** It might have a funny name, but bumblefoot is no laughing matter. A serious infection can spread to other tissue and bones and be fatal. A chicken will cut its foot; if the site gets infected, the bird's foot will swell. You'll sometimes see redness and a black or brown scab on the bottom of the foot. The most common symptoms are lameness and limping, but that means they've probably had the infection for a while.

Take your chicken to the vet. There's not a lot you can do to prevent bumblefoot, except to inspect your chicken's feet regularly, make sure their perch is splinter-free and if you notice a hen has a cut, pull out your handy first aid kit and wash and disinfect the wound.

- **Coccidiosis.** Coccidiosis is very common and sometimes deadly. It's a disease caused by a parasite. They can ingest it when they eat or drink food or water that's been contaminated by infected birds through their feces or by infected soil. One big issue is that one infected chicken can spread the disease for days before they show any symptoms. Chicks are most commonly infected, so you might think about using a medicated starter feed.

  Coccidiosis happens more in spring and summer when soil is moist and warm; the parasites find this the perfect environment to hang out until they can find a bird to infect. Symptoms include birds that look dirty or ruffles; weakness or inactivity; skin and combs are pale, no appetite and, in severe cases, yellow or foamy droppings.

  Treatment works quickly if the disease is caught early. You must treat every single bird in the flock, or you'll never contain an outbreak. Coccidiosis is usually treated by adding Amprolium to the water supply, but if the chickens aren't eating or drinking, it can be given orally. Treatment lasts seven days, and Amprolium can be given as a preventative–talk to your veterinarian. You can by Amprolium over the counter, and it's safe to eat eggs or meat from birds you've treated with it.

- **Fowlpox.** Fowlpox is a viral infection that spreads slowly. There are two forms: Wet and dry. With the wet form, the chicken gets plaques in their mouth and upper respiratory tract. If your chicken has the dry form, you'll see wart-like lesions that become thick scabs. It can cause depression, poor appetite and reduced growth or egg production. It lasts three to five weeks. Birds can get it from other birds, mosquitoes or contaminated equipment.

  There is a vaccine available for fowlpox. If you get an outbreak and your chickens are not vaccinated, you can vaccinate the other chickens against the disease. Fowlpox is rarely deadly; to help prevent it, practice mosquito prevention and eliminate standing water.

- **Newcastle Disease.** Newcastle Disease affects the chicken's respiratory system. You'll see breathing problems, murky eyes, nasal discharge, and laying will stop. Sometimes the bird's wings and legs will be paralyzed and their necks twisted. It's a virus that can be transmitted by contaminated equipment, shoes and clothes, but it's most commonly transmitted by free-flying birds.

There is no treatment for Newcastle disease, and it's incredibly contagious. Every single bird in the flock can come infected within three-or-four days as it spreads through the air. There is a vaccine for Newcastle disease, and adult birds usually recover, but most baby chicks will die.

There are, of course, a lot of other diseases that could affect your chickens, but these are the most common. You'll notice that cleanliness is a big part of disease prevention, so be sure to do all your daily and periodic chores as outlined in chapter three.

In addition to disease, chickens are affected by pests. The next section will outline those you're likely to encounter.

Common Pests

Now, microscopic bugs live on all of us, human or animal, which means chickens are no exception. To some parasites, a chicken is their whole world, and they live their whole lives on the bird. Let's explore the most common things crawling on your chickens, according to the University of California at Riverside.

- **Chicken Body Louse.** Don't worry, they don't feed on humans and will just drop off after a few hours. Not so with your chickens. These lice lay flat against the skin and are yellowish in color. You'll find them concentrated under the wings, but the live all over the chicken's body. They lay their eggs in white clusters on feathers.

  To spot an infestation, watch for: Dirty feathers near the vent, light comb color, lowered egg production, weight loss, appetite change, chickens pulling their feathers, irritated skin, bald spots, or actual bugs.

  To prevent lice: Keep wildlife away, make sure your chickens have a dust bath area that includes sand and diatomaceous earth, clean your coop adequately and quarantine any new chickens. Also, inspect your flock every one or two months–run your fingers over the skin of each bird to see if you see any bugs. If you see any signs, treat the entire flock.

  To get rid of lice, you can use over-the-counter medications, but most backyard chicken fanciers say they use diatomaceous earth–hold the chicken and gently apply the diatomaceous earth to their skin, stirring up as little dust as possible. Breathing in the dust can cause respiratory problems in humans and chickens, so wear a dust mask. Keep the chickens out of the coop for two hours so they aren't affected by flying dust.

Apply this treatment once a week for four weeks, and keep inspecting your birds to see if the number of parasites is decreasing.

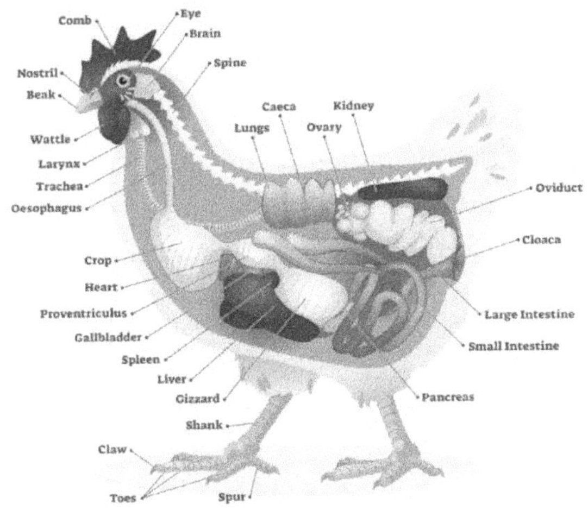

- **Sticktight Flea.** Sticktight fleas are dark brown and flat, and very visible on the comb and face of chickens. They embed themselves into the chicken's skin to feed. Females lay their eggs while they feed. These eggs fall to the ground and live on organic material in the chicken's litter or in soil. They can attach to dogs, cats, other pets and in rare cases, humans. If allowed to get out-of-hand, they can actually kill a chicken and they are especially dangerous to young birds. They can cause blindness by creating sores near the eyes.

To get rid of sticktight fleas, first get all the chickens out of the coop and lock them out. Remove all bedding and discard, and then scrub, scrub, scrub. While you wait for the coop to dry, treat the flock the same way you treat for lice. Wear gloves. You can remove the fleas with tweezers, and apply antibiotic ointment before dusting with diatomaceous earth. Again, the same precautions apply. Don't let the chickens breathe in the dust, and wear a face mask.

Repeat the entire process in 10 to 14 days, and a third time if necessary to break the flea life cycle.

- **Scaly Leg Mite.** Scaly leg mites are extremely tiny and they burrow under the scales of poultry leg and feet, where they cause irritation, swelling and crusty scabs. A chronic infestation of scaly leg mites can cause lameness and deformities.

Of course, clean out the coop thoroughly. You'll have to treat all the chickens. First, soak the legs and feet in warm water and dry gently, using a towel to exfoliate any dead, loose scale. Then, dip their feet in olive, linseed, vegetable or mineral oil to suffocate the mites. Then wipe off the oil and coat the area with petroleum jelly. Reapply the petroleum jelly several times a week until the chicken's legs return to normal. Keep in mind it might take several months for scaly leg mites to resolve.

- **Northern Fowl Mite.** The Northern fowl mite is the most common chicken parasite in North America. They're mostly found near the vent are of the chicken, in front of the cloaca. Mites have a very short life cycle, so they reproduce rapidly. While individual mites are tiny, the vent area will look dirty because of the eggs, feces, cast skins and mites–this means you have an infestation. They will get on humans who handle infested chickens, but they don't last long on a host that's not a bird.

Check for mites weekly. Total control means you'll have to use chemical pesticides. It's best if you consult a veterinarian to make sure exactly what types of mites you have and the best and healthiest method for getting and keeping them off of your flock.

- **Bed Bugs.** Bed bugs like to spend their time in cracks and crevices in your chicken coop. At night, they'll feast on the birds. Nest boxes, corners of your chicken house and chicken eggs should all be inspected for parasites or fecal spots.

  Adult bed bugs are reddish brown, wingless, and oval in shape. A female bed bug can lay up to 540 eggs during her life, and the population can double in 16 days. They give off an unpleasant odor, similar to stink bugs.

  They are a challenge to control, because they have become immune to many insecticides, and many are toxic to birds. Remove the birds, clean the coop thoroughly and disinfect. After you clean, use an insecticide *recommended by your vet* and apply it to all cracks, crevices, curtains, ceiling seems, nest boxes, slats, etc. Another alternative is to heat the coop–without the chickens in it–to 130 degrees for a few hours.

  Don't get bed bugs in your house! Change clothes and wash them in hot water and dry them on the highest heat. If you suspect bed bugs have entered your home, call a professional.

Worming

Chickens, like most animals, get worms. And some of them can cause a real problem with the health of the flock. The first step to take is to gather poop and take it to your vet for testing–they will do a smear slide or float test that will let you know if you need to worm your chickens. You never want to over-use worming medication, because the worms will eventually become resistant.

While worms can be treated by the chicken owner, as a beginner, it's best to use a vet at least the first time, because many of these worms can be contracted by humans. Your vet can demonstrate safe handling so you can do it yourself next time. Most people worm their chickens twice a year as a preventative.

Here's a rundown of chicken worms, how to get rid of them and how to prevent them:

- **Capillary Worms.** Capillary worms are small and thread-like, and you can't see them with the naked eye, so grab a magnifying glass. There are several types of capillary worms that live in the crop, intestines and ceca. A bird can die from a severe infestation. Chickens get these worms by eating slugs or earthworms.

Your chicken will become anemic and weak, and have a pale comb, decreased appetite, look very thin and can sometimes have diarrhea. Consult your veterinarian about treatment and do not eat the eggs for the withdrawal period.

- **Gape Worms.** Gape worms are nasty, nasty, nasty. The live in the windpipe of chickens and feed on the blood they get from small blood vessels. With a severe infestation, they can cause partial obstruction of the windpipe, leaving your chicken gasping for air. They are "Y" shaped, and this is actually the male and female locked together in permanent copulation.

  Infected birds will look shabby, and may cough, gasp for air and eat less. The worm eggs are excreted in the chicken poop, meaning the next bird will get it. Call your vet. The entire flock will have to be treated.

- **Tapeworms.** You've probably heard of these, as people get them as well. They're flat, segmented worms that look like a ribbon. They're easy to see in the poop. Fortunately, they're not very common in chickens.

They leach nutrients from the bird, causing weight loss and depression. If young chickens get them, their growth can be stunted. Tapeworms are a vicious cycle–each shedded segment contains and egg that can be eaten by beetles, slugs and snails which are eaten by the chicken. Again, call your vet to treat the flock.

- **Roundworms.** Roundworms live their entire life cycle in the chicken, and she'll shed the eggs in her poop, another chicken will peck at it and then become infected. They live in the small intestine and are the common worm infestation in chickens. They can be seen by the naked eye, and can grow to a length of up to six inches.

  Roundworms cause decreased appetite, pale comb and wattles, diarrhea, wasting (wasting is progressive weakness, regression of comb, paleness, enlarged abdomen, emaciation and death) and can stunt growth. In severe cases, they can cause intestinal blockage, which means death. If you see roundworms, call your vet.

- **Eye Worms.** Also known as Manson's eye worm, these worms used to be considered a tropical disease, but they've recently been found in the warmer areas of the United States.

This worm lives in the eye of an infected chicken, and is usually caused by infected cockroaches, but infected feed, bedding or poop can spread it.

Look for a cheese-type discharge from the eye; it can cause the eyelids to stick together. The hen will scratch at the eye and have a decreased appetite. If untreated, this worm can cause blindness. Again, call your vet if you notice any symptoms.

- **Cecal Worms.** Like roundworms, cecal worms live their entire life cycle inside the chicken. They infest the ceca of the chicken, and very common. These mostly infect turkeys, but can be passed to chickens if they are raised with turkeys, so never raise turkeys and chickens together. Again, talk to your vet.

Prevention is really the best option when it comes to the health of your flock. Again, cleanliness rears its head and it can't be overstated – it's really the main key to keeping healthy chickens.

Keep coops and all areas clean, and don't let waste pile up. And diatomaceous earth is practically a miracle-worker for keeping down parasites. They love warm, damp places, so keep your run and the areas around it as dry as you can. If you see mud puddles, fill them with dirt, sand and pebbles. And keep grass short.

There is a natural wormer called Verm-X that is used by many a chicken raiser to control parasites, but check with both other chicken owners and your vet. Some worm their chickens every six months, but Since resistance to pharmaceutical wormers is a real problem, you may only want to worm your chickens if they become infested.

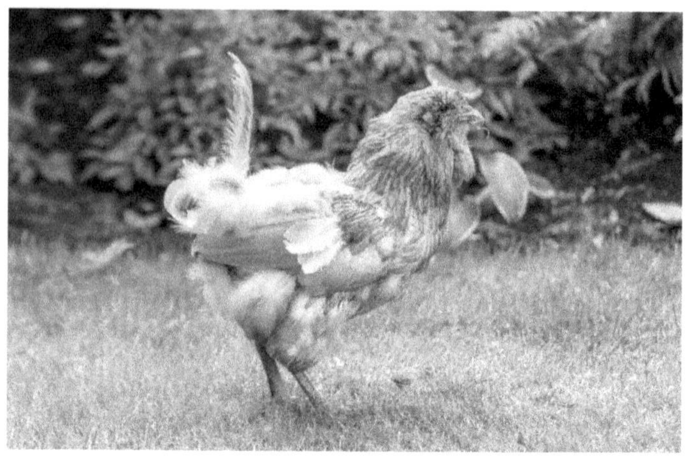

Molting

All chickens molt. In birds older than a year, they usually molt in late summer or autumn to refresh their plumage for the cold winter. While they molt, hens use their energy to grow feathers rather than laying eggs.

Chickens molt because over time, their plumage gets dull, broken and shabby looking. You probably won't notice this unless you compare a molted chicken with one that hasn't yet molted. Basically, molting helps your chicken survive winter. Broken and worn out feathers can't insulate your hen against wind, rain and snow. Molting gets rid of these old feathers, and replaces them with new, tight feathers to better protect your bird.

There are three types of molts: With a hard molt, all of the feathers are lost quickly. With a soft molt, the feathers drop and regrow gradually. Sometimes, the only way your know your chicken is going through a soft molt is because she's stopped laying. Young birds will go through a series of molts as they grow their adult feathers. They won't do a "regular" molt until the next Fall, when they're 15-to-18 months old.

Your chicken's molt type depends on their genes. Commercial chicken factories breed for a hard molt because it's over quickly. Natural molting on a far or a backyard is brought on by the shorter days leading to winter, but it can also be triggered by other things. Factory farms will deprive a chicken of food for a couple of days or water for a day, to get them to molt all at once, because it's easier for them to manage.

Molting hens will lay few eggs, if any, while molting and this is completely normal. It takes a few weeks or more for a chicken to complete a molt. As you'll see in the section on alternative health care, there are ways to move the molt along by adding more protein to their diet. Some flock owners report that they halved egg loss time with this method.

So, does a molting hen need special attention? YES! Feathers are about 85 percent protein, so it's really important to give them high-protein food or to add additional protein to their diet. You can switch to a feed that has a minimum of 18 percent protein, or give them game bird feed, which is 20-to-22 percent protein. Don't keep feeding the additional protein after they molt, as it can damage their health. Use it during molting only.

And while they're molting, give them only high-protein snacks. No "junk" food.

Molting is very stressful for your chickens because they need all that extra protein. Moting is also considered the end of the hen's laying cycle, so when she starts laying eggs again, it's the start of another egg-laying year. And just a tip: Don't buy your chicken a sweater just because your chicken looks bald and pathetic. They don't need sweaters. If you're still tempted, thinking how cute Henrietta would look, keep in mind that they can keep your chicken from regulating their body temperature, trap moisture under the skin (the lice and mites will love that!), interfere with their natural preening and makes them easy prey–hey, a handle!

Traditional Health Care

Traditional chicken health care includes vaccinations. No one can tell you that you must vaccinate your flock–it's a personal decision. Under the next section on alternative health care, you'll read about why some choose not to have their birds vaccinated. Some buy the vaccine and do it themselves. You can buy vaccines online. These are the vaccines recommended by vets and when they're given.

Information in this section came from thefrugalchicken.com and the Merck Veterinary Manual. Note that if you plan to raise chickens for meat, you can't butcher poultry that have received vaccinations–you must wait 15 days to 60 days, depending on the vaccination. Be sure to consult your vet.

- **Marek's Disease Vaccine.** This is usually given to day old chicks, to both broilers and layers. Most hatcheries will do it for a small fee, but if you buy from a local feed store or farmer, you'll have to have your vet do the vaccinating. It's given below the skin, in the breast of the chick. Chicks are extremely fragile, and there's a possibility of injury, so make sure whoever is doing it is expert. You can buy this vaccine online without a prescription.
- **Newcastle's Disease and Infectious Bronchitis.** This particular vaccine is normally given to chickens between 14 days and 21 days old. This vaccine requires a prescription, so talk to your vet about it; they can also tell you dosages. This vaccination is administered in their water, and carries as number of warnings, including the fact that this vaccine can cause inflammation of the eyelids in people that lasts up to three days.

- **Infectious Bursal Disease.** This is another vaccine that goes into the water, and again, for chickens aged between 14 days and 21 days old. This a disease of the bursa seen in young chickens. On a chicken, the bursa is an organ that has no human counterpart. The closest human equivalent would be bone marrow. A healthy bursa means a healthy chicken immune system. They get watery diarrhea, dehydration and ruffled feathers. The death rate is usually low, but a really strong strain can cause a mortality rate of 60 percent or higher.
- **Encephalomyelitis.** This is a nasty viral infection that, in a severe outbreak, can kill more than 50 percent of your chickens. It causes tremors, ataxia (a lack of coordination), weakness, and eventually, paralysis. This is given to chicks at 10-to-12 weeks old in the wing web. The wing web is a network of interlocking parts that give a feather its smooth appearance. If you pull the wing out from a chicken, you can see the webbing.
- **Fowlpox.** This is another vaccine given in the wing web at the same age as the encephalomyelitis vaccine.
- **Laryngotracheitis**. Laryngotracheitis is a highly contagious virus. This is very serious, so if one chicken gets it, it's likely the rest will and you will have no choice but to put the entire

flock down. Like most of the other vaccines, this is given to chicks between 10 week and 12 weeks of age by drops in the eyes.

- **Mycoplasma gallisepticum.** This disease is caused by bacteria, and turns into a chronic respiratory disease. It can enter the eggs and infect newly-hatched chicks. Chicks are vaccinated between 10 weeks and 14 weeks old, and is given via eye drops or a spray, but an injectable vaccine is available online–please consult your vet before using it.

Traditional chicken health care can also include the use of pesticides and other chemicals in and around your coop. Research and explore all the facts before making a decision about what's right for you and your flock.

Alternative Health Care

Is it possible to raise a healthy flock without vaccines and antibiotics? Before modern medicine, it was the only way you *could* raise chickens or any livestock. In chapter four, you learned about dietary supplements: Grit, calcium, apple cider vinegar, electrolytes, probiotics, diatomaceous earth, molasses and protein. These are all used by chicken fanciers who prefer a natural method for pest and disease control.

Home remedies should be used to prevent health problems or address minor injuries, advises hobbyfarms.com, but not full-blown disease. You can't just treat the symptoms, so be sure to talk to a vet.

Those who prefer to raise their chicken "naturally" recommend the following:

- **To Stop Bleeding: Instead of styptic powder or pencil**
    - Take a black or green tea bag and soak it in warm water. Wring it out, and then apply to the wound until bleeding stops.
    - Apply white vinegar to constrict blood vessels and stop the bleeding.
    - Wrap an ice cube in a damp cloth and hold it against the wound.
    - Grind dried yarrow to a fine powder, and sprinkle it into the wound. When the wound stops bleeding, clean it and apply more yarrow powder as a dressing.
- **To Prevent Bugs: Instead of chemical insecticides**
    - Sprinkle a coating of lime on hen house floors and runs twice a year or more to prevent mite and louse

infestations, and don't let wild birds to nest near your coop.

- Diatomaceous earth strikes again! Sprinkle in nest boxes, on roosts and all over the floor to help with mites. You can also hang bunches of wormwood in the coop or add garlic to the chicken's food or water.
- Use water infused with garlic juice and essential oils to kill mites. Make a spray and use it under their wings. The best essential oils for this are: Bay, cinnamon, clove, lavender, spearmint and thyme. Use only a few drops of oil. After you spray your hens, dust them with diatomaceous earth–remember to use food grade only, and avoid their eyes and yours! Wear a dust mask and use a light touch with the earth.
- For scaly leg mites, soak the chicken's legs in soapy water with a splash of ammonia. When the crusty stuff is soft, scrub the legs gently with an old toothbrush or nail brush. Dry the legs and apply a thick layer of petroleum jelly or a eucalyptus-infused ointment (these are typically used for human colds). Or, you can use coconut oil, or mix one-half cup petroleum jelly with

two tablespoons of sulphur powder. You should repeat this every few days. And make sure to scrub the henhouse!

- **To Ease Respiratory Symptoms: Instead of prescription medication**
    - Add several drops of peppermint or eucalyptus essential oil to a quart of boiling water. Carefully and securely, hold your hen over the pot. Make sure the steam isn't too hot and then put a towel over her head. Hold her there for five-to-10 minutes and repeat as needed.
    - Instead of using essential oils, you can use one teaspoon of rosemary and one teaspoon of thyme–fresh or dried work–to a quart pot of water and bring it to a boil. Remove from the heat, cover it, and let it steep for five minutes. Then, hold the chicken over the steaming water, just like above.
    - Make a solution of one teaspoon of VetRx (a commercial product that has Canada balsam, camphor, origanum, and rosemary) in one cup of warm water. Drip it into the chicken's

nostrils. You can also add a few drops of VetRx to their drinking water.

- Finely chop and crush three cloves of garlic and mix it with a big dash of apple cider vinegar. Add to the drinking water at a ratio of two tablespoons of mixture to one gallon of water.

- **To help molting hens**

You've read about molting so you know there's a real incentive to move the molting process along: Hens don't lay until it's over. Here's what to do:

- To add a big dose of antioxidants and omega-3 fatty acids, add linseed meal or flax seeds to their feed.
- Give chickens high-protein dried cat food–a handful a day.
- Add dill, fennel, kelp, nettles, cleavers and garlic to your chicken feed.

And what about acupuncture? The Chi Institute in Reddick, Florida, specializes in Traditional Chinese Veterinary Medicine. But, you don't have to go to Florida. Search the web; some acupuncturists who treat people also are certified for animals. Or, ask your vet or a like-minded chicken fancier.

In 2016, the institute demonstrated how to relax a chicken into egg-laying with just one needle! Out it plopped! There are 350 acupuncture sites in animals. This is great news for those with egg-bound birds.

Some chicken fanciers use homeopathy. It's a bit controversial; some believe it works, others think it's total hocum.

Homeopathy is an alternative medicine modality that involves plant, mineral and/or animal extracts. They are diluted with water to particular potencies. They can be used to keep your flock healthy, but their probably best used after you have more chicken-handling experience.

The American Institute of Homeopathy tells us that the word homeopathy comes from the Greek, and means "like disease," meaning that "like cures like." Often, homeopathic remedies will contain very diluted samples of the disease their treating.

If you like the thought of treating your flock with homeopathy, find a holistic vet. If you use a human holistic doctor who practices homeopathy, they will often also treat animals, so ask.

Homeopathic remedies come in capsules, granules, tablets and liquid tinctures; you may have to experiment to know which form is easiest for you to administer.

CHAPTER SEVEN

COMMON PROBLEMS

As you've read, chickens are all different and have different personalities, but some problems are common to all flocks. Here are some things that can go wrong:

- **Rooster attack.** The rooster might be king of the chicken yard, but if they start attacking people, it's time to do something. Roosters are very sensitive to anything they perceive as aggressive. So even wearing big boots or swinging a bucket could seem like a challenge to these macho birds. And, as the man of the yard and the protector of the flock, he will refuse to back down.

  If your rooster is attacking, catch him and then hold him if he starts being aggressive. Be sure to wear protective clothing, and hold him until he calms down and realizes you're in charge.

Be the alpha chicken! And let them know you're the real boss of the roost when he's young, rather than trying to teach an old chicken new tricks.

- **Feather loss.** Your chickens are probably molting, and if they are, you'll be able to see new feathers coming in. But, also check for mites or lice and check them over to make sure there's not something else going on.

- **Pecking and cannibalism.** It's not pleasant to think about and certainly horrible to see, but pecking and cannibalism can be a serious problem. Cannibalistic chickens peck at each other's feathers, toes, heads, and bodies. Chickens naturally imitate each other, so once this type of behavior starts, it spreads quickly through the flock. If you don't catch it early, injuries and death can mean the loss of a large part of your flock.

  Kansas State University Extension says there are a number of things that can lead to cannibalism: Excessive lighting, overheating, poor nutrition, overcrowding and introducing bird that didn't grow up together. It's a difficult problem for a chicken owner to deal with, so hire an expert to can trim the beaks of the cannibal birds. Also remove any injured birds, dim the coop lighting, and provide some scratch. Try hanging CDs, DVDs or other shiny items at varying heights so the birds are distracted and have something else to peck.

- **Hens stop laying.** As you've read, chickens stop laying when they molt, but the most common reasons are shorter days, improper nutrition, age, disease or stress.

  Hens require at least 14 hours of daylight to keep up egg production, so as the days grow shorter, provide artificial light in the coop. Make sure you're feeding nutritionally complete food, and take any seemingly-ill chickens to the vet.

- **Eating their eggs.** Eggs are delicious, and hens feel the same way about them. Once they taste an egg, it's pretty much impossible to break hens of the egg-eating habit. Make sure to collect eggs at least twice a day, and check the coop for any broken eggs; clean them up immediately. If you do have an egg eating hen, you'll have to remove her from the flock.

- **Won't lay eggs in the coop.** I'm sure your coop is lovely and comfortable, but still, your hens won't lay their eggs there. This is most common with free-range birds who can go anywhere they want, which means they can lay their eggs where they want as well. Once a hen finds a place it likes to lay, they are stubborn and rarely change their minds. So, you're pretty much going to have to live with your hens doing their own thing.

- **Broodiness in hens.** Even if they lay unfertilized eggs, a hen's natural instinct is to sit on and hatch them. A broody hen has hormonal changes brought on by a nest full of eggs, and some will "go broody" even without a full nest–Cochins and Silkies are known for going broody and Leghorns rarely do, says the Oregon State University Extension.

  Hens don't lay when they're broody. Reduce broodiness by collecting eggs at least daily. If you have a hen who won't leave her nest for days, remove her and deny her access for a few days. This should stop the broodiness and start her laying eggs again.

- **Mites and lice.** The subject of mites and lice has been covered thoroughly, but the importance of detecting and preventing them can't be overemphasized. These pests can damage a flock. As you've read, sanitation and cleanliness are the essential keys to controlling lice and mites. And be sure your hens have diatomaceous earth to roll around in.

These are the common problems encountered by backyard chicken enthusiasts, and next you'll be able to learn from the experience of others…

CHAPTER EIGHT

CHICKEN-KEEPING MISTAKES TO AVOID

While all the talk of diseases, parasites and attacking roosters might give you pause, most people who keep chickens say they're actually pretty easy to take care of. But here's a list of mistakes to avoid.

- Don't bring your chickens home before you finish their coop
- Don't melt the brooder with a heat lamp (this can also cause a fire!)
- Don't forget to check for pasty butt
- Don't leave your chicken feed out so rats can get it
- Don't make your coop impossible to keep clean
- Don't leave your coop open at night–you're just creating a raccoon buffet!

- Don't get more chickens than you have space for
- Don't get the wrong chicken breeds for your particular climate
- Don't let your flock roam your neighborhood
- Don't let your birds eat poisonous plants
- Don't buy meat birds with a plan to butcher them
- Don't keep a rooster illegally in a city setting
- Don't make your mobile coop too heavy to move
- Don't put chicks with adult chickens–the larger chickens will peck the chicks to death
- Don't forget to add or put out grit for your chickens
- Don't forget to provide diatomaceous earth for "bathing"
- Don't forget to give your chickens sunshine and shade
- Don't forget to put nesting boxes in a quiet spot–a relaxed chicken will lay more eggs

In addition, attinable-sustainable.net offers more errors to avoid if you want happy and healthy chickens:

- Make sure to really protect your coop from predators. They are very, very clever. Try concrete blocks and wire. Raise the level of your hen house with concrete cinder blocks and use fine-gauge or overlapped wire.

- Store food properly to keep it clean and dry. If you just store feed bags, the contents are subject not only to damp and mold, but to the chickens themselves and their predators.
- Do everything you can to discourage mosquitos. Use a chicken waterer that has a cover and don't allow water to stand on your property.
- In keeping with having a coop that's easy to clean, most backyard chicken farmers say that if you're building a chicken coop and nest boxes, be sure to add an access door that will let you gather eggs without entering the hen house. This way, you don't have to step through a bunch of hens who think you might have a tasty treat for them.
- Don't think you need nesting boxes for each hen. Sometimes hens like to share boxes, so start with one box for every two hens.
- Nesting boxes shouldn't be flat, because your hens will roost there and poop all over. Make them with a sloped top.

Some of these items repeat information in earlier chapters, but they all bear repeating. There's no better advice than that given by the voice of experience! Now, let's do a brief exploration of raising chickens for meat and what you do with old chickens when they stop laying.

CHAPTER NINE

RAISING CHICKENS FOR MEAT AND WHAT TO DO WITH OLD CHICKENS

This book is about raising chickens for eggs, although some of the chickens listed in chapter two are multi-purpose. Meat chickens, also known as broilers, are larger, bulkier breeds. They have more muscle tone than layers, and can be both male and female. Meat chickens lay fewer eggs than laying hens.

If you want to raise them from chicks, you would buy baby broiler chicks, which grow to maturity at the age of eight weeks to 12 weeks; that's when their meat is the tenderest and most juicy. They need a very high protein diet, so you start with a chick broiler starter feed with 22-to-24 percent protein, then a chick grower feed with 20 percent protein and finish with a chick finisher feed at about 18 percent protein.

The most popular meat chicken is the white Cornish Cross, a mixture of a Cornish rooster and a white Plymouth Rock hen. They're known as the "Meat Kings" because they are very efficient at converting feed to muscle. At as early as eight-to-10 weeks, they can be sold as broilers; they also can be kept longer and sold as roasters.

Aside from a difference in feed, you raise meat chickens almost the same way as layers. At around six to eight weeks, though, you'll start weighing a meat chicken to see if their large enough to slaughter (a minimum of five-to-six pounds). If you want roasters, wait a few more weeks.

And, at around three weeks old, you should move meat chickens to a bigger coop, and this is where you start feeding the chickens the grower feed.

Breed matters when it comes to
the edible portion of meat: 75 percent for white hybrids,
70 percent for colored hybrids and 65 percent for heritage breeds.

What To Do With Old Chickens

So, just what do you do with an old hen who no longer lays? Hens start laying at about five months, and the first two years of their life are their most productive. After that, their egg production declines each year until it stops completely when they're about seven years old.

With the growth of backyard chicken keeping, cities are finding people abandoning chickens in parks, releasing them into the wild, taken to animal shelters or just randomly abandoned.

There are a number of alternatives to abandonment, according to thecapecoop.com.

- **Contact a local farmer and see if they want the chicken(s).** If they take them, they'll likely be using it to eat or to use their meat in animal feed. This means your chicken goes on to a productive afterlife, humanely slaughtered and feeding people.
- **Slaughter the chicken yourself.** Instructions to do this follow this section, although backyard chicken raisers prefer to use the word "process," rather than "slaughter."
- **Let them live out their natural life.** If you raised the bird, named it, petted it, held it, it might be impossible for you to even entertain the thought of your chicken becoming someone's or something's meal. Old chickens are great bug hunters, and they'll teach your young hens about life in the flock. Young hens will learn by watching: How to build a nest, how to roost and night and how to interact

with other chickens. Old hens can also be used to sit on fertilized eggs.

Keep in mind that older chickens are more prone to disease, they don't move as fast, and they may have trouble getting to high roosts. If you decide to "process" your old chicken, you can eat it, but old birds are tough, so you'll use her for making soup or stew, rather than roasting. If a bird is sick and needs to be put down, you can kill and then bury it rather than completing the full processing steps.

How To Slaughter A Chicken

Note: Those sensitive to graphic verbal depictions or animal slaughter or those who intend to keep their chickens until their natural death should skip this section.

No matter if it's a meat chicken or an old laying hen, you'll do everything the same way. There are several ways to kill a chicken. One is by breaking its neck with your bare hands, but you have to have serious grip strength for older birds. Snap the spinal cord behind the skull.

You can also break a chicken's neck with a broom. With this method, you hold the bird by it's leg, and lay it on the floor on it's breast, beak-side down.

Put the pole over the bird's neck close to the skull, place a foot on either side of the head, and pull firmly and steadily upward until the neck is dislocated.

With both of these methods, feel the gap between the skull and the end of the neck to make sure it's broken. And, also with all of these methods listed, the chicken will spasm and violently flap, but it's unconscious.

Decapitation with an axe or hatchet is an alternative method to using the killing cone mentioned below. This method is quite old-fashioned and not recommended because you can easily cut yourself or injuring another person if someone is helping you by holding the bird.

Now, for the most-used method of killing and processing a chicken, according to thespruce.com as well as other chicken-related sites:

Step 1: Set up Your Processing Station. You'll need:

- **Two or more *very sharp* knives**, four-to-six inches in length
- **A "pinning knife"** for removing pin feathers
- **A Killing cone**, also called a restraining cone or slaughter cone: This is a special metal cone for poultry.

You can buy this at a feed store or online.

- **Buckets.** You'll put a bucket under the cone to catch the blood and feathers. You'll need another for the internal organs and other discarded pieces.
- **A steady supply of water,** like from a garden hose. You'll rinse tools, your hands and the chicken after each step.
- **Gloves** make the process easier.
- **Old clothes,** because it's messy.
- **A table,** covered with a plastic tarp to eviscerate the hen.
- **A scalding tank** made from a really large stockpot or turkey fryer. Fill it with water, and put it over a burner. The pot must be large enough to dunk the birds in and swirl them around. This will scald them and make plucking much easier.
- **A thermometer** to make sure the water is hot enough.
- **A cooler** with ice and water where you can place the birds after processing.
- **Paper towels** for cleaning up.
- **A cutting surface** like a cutting board.
- **Plastic storage bags,** one or two gallon size.

Step 2: Grab Your Bird. Hold it by the feet and let it hang upside down and place the bird in the killing cone.

Step 3: Cut the artery and vein.

- **Pull the chicken's head** through the bottom of the cone and hold it.
- **Using your sharpest knife**, cut just behind where the tendon attaches to the beak and tongue–find the hard piece of cartilage behind the jaw attachment. Sever the jugular vein and carotid artery. No hesitation now! Make a deep, firm slice on both sides of the neck.
- **Pull the head down firmly** and allow the blood to drain into a bucket. **Warning:** At this point, the chicken will kick and jerk. Just stay calm. This is normal. The bird is unconscious and unaware. Drain the blood completely.

Step 4: Scald the chicken

- **Make sure your water temperature is 135 F to 140F.**
- **Remove the bird from the cone**, and hold it gently by the feet or legs.

- **Dunk the bird headfirst into the tank**, gently swirling it around and up-and-down, and be sure to get all the leg feathers into the water.
- **Check the scald.** Rub your hand or fingers on the leg feathers, against the grain, and then pluck a large feather. If the feathers come out easily, you're done with the scald. If they don't, keep scalding and checking. Just don't scald too long, or it will damage the chicken's skin. This will make the skin tear easily and a long scaling will also affect the amount of time the chicken can be stored.

Step 5: Pluck the feathers

- **If you can, hang the bird by its feet.** Put a pail underneath so the feathers can fall into it and you can easily rinse off the chicken after plucking.
- **Remove the feathers** by rubbing your fingers and thumb against the feather's grain to get the smaller feathers without plucking. For the larger feathers, pluck only a few at a time to avoid damaging the skin.

Step 6: Get rid of pin feathers

- **Scrape the pinning knife** very gently along the surface of the skin to remove the pin feathers. It wasn't that long ago that even chickens purchased in a supermarket still had pinfeathers that the cook would singe off on a gas stove.
- **Rinse the bird** to remove any loose feathers.

Step 7: Remove the preen gland

- **If not removed**, the preen gland will ruin the meat. Cut above the gland and cut to the bone. Slide your knife along the bone and end with the tail. Make sure there's no glandular tissue (it's yellow) left on the hen.

Step 8: Remove the feet

- **Straighten the leg** and cut between the joints to remove the feet.

Step 9: Remove the head, trachea, esophagus and crop

- **You might want to use a cleaver for this.** Cut through the bone to remove the head.
- **Slit the skin** along the back of the neck and slide it down, then separate

the trachea and esophagus all the way to where they enter the body.

- **You should feel the crop.** If you starved the bird before slaughter, it will be empty. But either way, loosen the crop from the skin and carefully pull it free of the body.
- **Leave the trachea, esophagus and crop hanging free.**

Step 10: Open the body cavity

- **Insert your knife about an inch above the vent.** Slit the skin open to the breastbone. Carefully cut around the vent and pull it free–the intestines will follow. **Warning:** When cutting, be careful not to cut the intestines.

Step 11: Eviscerate, Chill and Store the Chicken

- **Reach into the bird.** Run your hand along the sides of the ribs to free the entrails. Then find the gizzard–a hard, round organ. Pull it out and the entrails will follow, and if you performed step nine, the trachea, esophagus and crop should also come out. If not, remove them separately.

- **Go back in and get the lungs.** You can find them by putting your hand in the body cavity and follow the outline of the ribs to the spine. Keep going until you don't feel any more lung tissue, which is squishy. You can also buy a tool called a "lung scraper."
- **Remove the neck** by cutting the muscle tissue around the bone, bending it and then breaking the bone through.
- **Chill the bird** in the ice water for an hour. After chilling, pat the bird dry with paper towels and store it in a large plastic zipper bag in the refrigerator.

The meat should age in the refrigerator for a few days before eating or freezing, so the muscles go through rigor mortis and then relax. Birds that haven't aged will be tough and hard to eat. For broilers and old hens, age 36 hours, for 10-to-12-week-old chickens, age for 48 hours.

When you do your final cleanup, be sure to wash everything you used, including knives, thermometer, pails, cone, table cover, etc. with a diluted bleach solution and then rinse with clean water.

So, there you have it. Not the most pleasant of chores, but it's a great way to experience the full chicken lifecycle from coop to table without waste.

Let's move along, and hear from the voice of experience. A couple of chicken owners share their stories and tips.

CHAPTER TEN

CHICKEN LORE: CHICKEN RAISERS SHARE THEIR EXPERIENCES AND TIPS

Nothing beats experience. You've read about coops, choosing chickens, how to care for them in sickness and in health and what they do with the chickens at the end of their "useful" lives.

First, let's hear from Damian. She's kept chickens for 10 years, but actually acquired her first chicken when she was in college.

"I had chickens in the mid-70s," she said. "Someone gave me a chicken because they knew I love animals. I'm fascinated by them because they each have their own personalities and quirks, which I didn't know before I had them. They are all unique. I ended up with 10 laying chickens; I built my first chicken coop when I was 19." She had a roommate who wanted chickens, they had a big yard, so she thought, "why not?"

Damian ended up living in Oakland, California, where she won third place in a backyard chicken coop building contest!

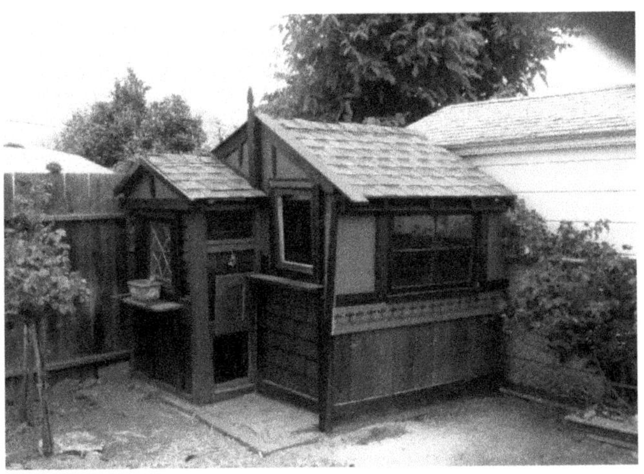

Damian's prize-winning coop

She's had Rhode Island Reds, Silkies, Plymouth Rocks, Buffs and a Mille Fleur d'Uccle bantam. For beginning chicken owners, she recommends Rhode Island Reds, Buffs, Plymouth Rock and Silkies.

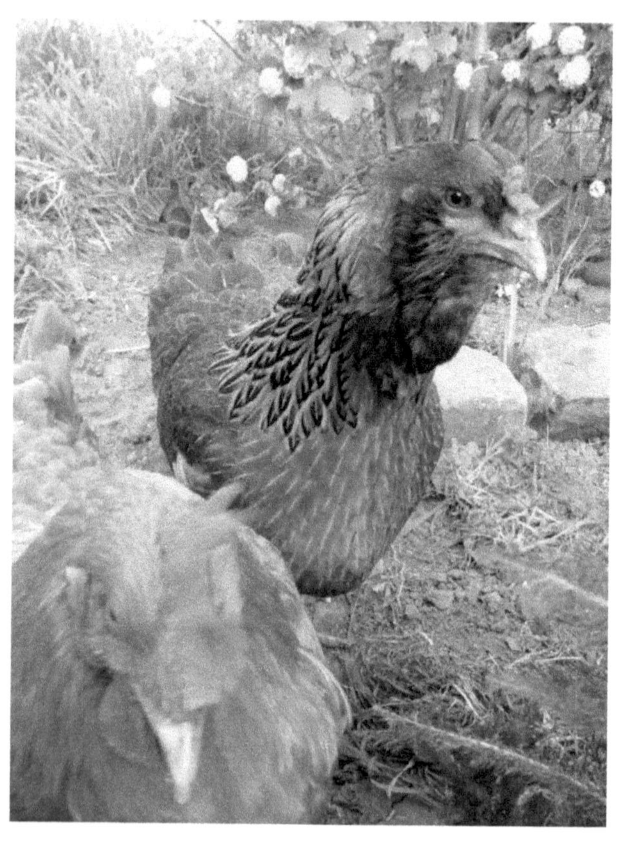

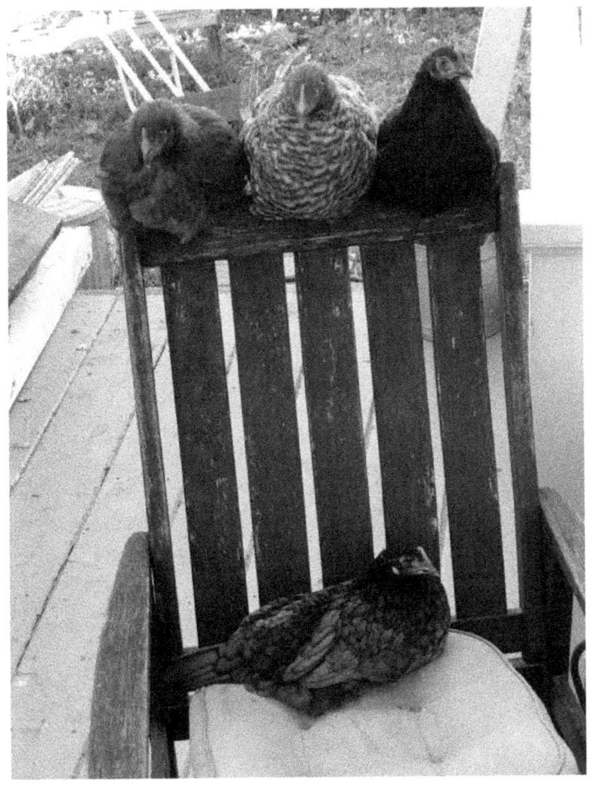

Damian advises the beginning chicken farmer to be especially careful about predators. "Just make sure they have shelter from predators. One night I forgot to close the coop and then had to watch as a raccoon killed a chicken before I could chase it away. Have you ever heard a chicken screaming? It's horrible." Let those be words to the wise!

Her chickens have mostly been free-range, and she reiterates what you've read about: Free range chickens will destroy a garden with their scratching.

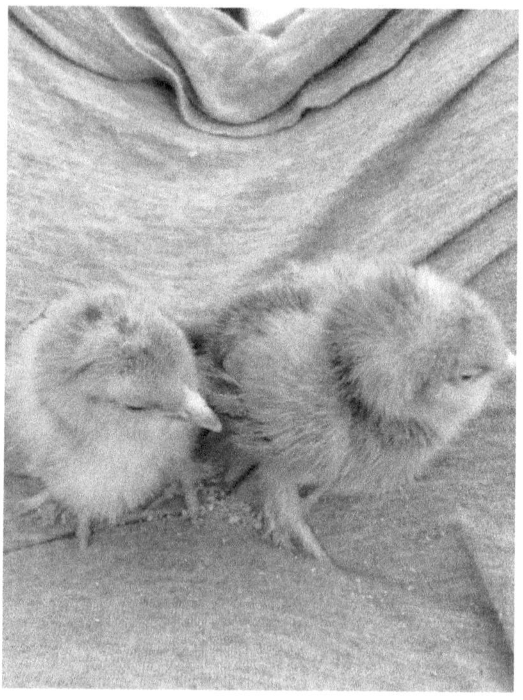

Damian's chickens are basically pets that lay eggs. She's raised most of her chickens by hatching fertilized eggs. "You get really close to them when you raise them from chicks, especially." She built her own brooder box and kept the chicks in the house until they got their adult feathers. As adults, the chickens were kept out of the house.

She has no regrets about raising chickens.

Now, let's talk to Andre. He got his first chicken 30 years ago. "We got our first hen when we saw her at the Little Farm near Tilden Park (Berkeley, California). Apparently, people drop off their unwanted hens thinking the Little Farm will take them in. They don't, so they're left to fend for themselves and usually end up as a raccoon meal.

"So, we caught this hen and brought her home. She hung around outside and sometimes came in. We have a picture of her sitting on the dishwasher door. At some point, we started finding eggs in the laundry basket. They tasted better than any eggs we've tried before, so we were hooked!"

Andre said that in addition to the great eggs, there are other advantages to raising chickens. "They eat leftovers, which we had plenty of when our four kids were small, and then they turn the scraps into fertilizer for our garden. It's also fun to watch them and listen to the sounds they make as they settle down for the night."

He raises Rhode Island Reds, Amerucanas and Australorps. For the beginner, he recommends the Rhode Island Reds and Australorps. "My wife like the way the Amerucanas look, but they curtail egg laying in the fall," he says.

His advice for the novice is to get a feeder that keeps out rats and mice; "They consume a lot of food, they stink and they make neighbors grumpy." His biggest challenge when he first started was trying to keep the chickens in their enclosure and from destroying plants.

Andre sells his excess eggs, and when his chickens stop laying, he makes chicken soup or stew.

So, the experiences of two different people with different outlooks. For Damian, her chickens are pets who produce delicious eggs for her own use, while for Andre, they are a source of both food and income.

CHAPTER ELEVEN

A CHICKEN RAISING GLOSSARY

Just as with any hobby chicken enthusiasts have their own language. This glossary should give you all the terms and definitions you need to navigate the world of chicken raising, from the Indiana State Poultry Association, Mother Earth News and Poultryhub.

ADDLED: An egg whose contents are decomposing because the embryo has died.

AIR CELL: The air space usually found at the large end of an egg.

ALBUMEN: The white of the egg.

AXIAL FEATHERS: These are the longer wing feathers that grow from the middle section; they're exposed when the hen's wing is folded under.

BANTAM: A small domestic chicken, often a miniature version of a larger breed.

BEARD: The most common terms for the feathers under some chicken's chins. Breeds that have beards include Americanas and varieties of D'Uccles.

BIDDY: An affectionate term for a hen.

BLOOM: The natural coating an egg is laid with; a thin film that seals the eggshell's pores, helping them stay fresh and keep out bacteria.Washing removes the bloom.

BROILER: A chicken raised for meat. They are processed at age seven weeks to 12 weeks, or when it reaches two-and-a-half-to-three pounds in weight.

BROODER BOX: A temperature-controlled, heated box used for raising newly hatched chicks.

BROODING: The process of caring for newly-hatched chicks.

BROODY HEN: A hen that is intent on sitting on a nest and hatching eggs. Broody hens are often used to hatch eggs of other chicken, or to hatch purchased fertilized eggs.

BROODING PERIOD: The period in a young chicken's life between hatching until they grow their adult feathers.

BUMBLEFOOT: An infection on the sole of a chicken's foot.

BUTTERCUP COMB: A comb that has a single leader near the beak that leads into a comb with evenly spaced points; it looks like a crown on the bird's head.

CANDLING: The process of shining light through an egg to determine if it is fertilized.

CANNIBALISM: When birds attack and eat members of their own flock.

CAPE: The long, narrow feathers between a chicken's neck and back. These are often the most colorful feathers on your chicken.

CAPON: Male chickens that have been castrated at four-to-eight months old. They weigh five-to-nine pounds and they produce more white meat and have higher fat content than other chickens.

CHICK: A newly hatched or very young chicken.

CHICK TOOTH: A hard tooth-like structure at the end of a chick's beak. It's also known as an egg tooth since chicks use it to break through the eggshell when hatching.

CHRONIC RESPIRATORY DISEASE (CRD): A disease of chickens indicated by sneezing and breathing difficulties. It's usually controlled with antibiotics in feed or drinking water.

CLOACA: The opening in the rear of a chicken. The intestinal, urinary and reproductive tracts empty from the cloaca. Also commonly called the vent.

CLUTCH: A group of eggs in one nest.

COCCIDIOSIS: When chickens contract this disease, the parasite Coccidia has invaded the intestinal tract. It spreads between chickens by contact with feces or ingestion of infected tissue.

COCK: A male chicken more than one year old.

COCKEREL: A male chicken less than a year old.

COMB: The fleshy growth on the top of a chicken's head. Combs are larger on male chickens and are typically red.

COOP: An enclosure or housing structure built for chickens.

CROP: Part of a chicken's digestive system. It's located at the base of the neck. It stores food after eating but before digestion.

CULL: Identification and removal of non-productive birds.

DOWN: Soft, fine and fluffy feathers on chickens; chicks have only down before they grow in their adult feathers.

DUST BATH: This can refer to a vessel with diatomaceous earth and sand that chickens use, or it can describe the chicken's behavior of bathing with dust to help get rid of mites and parasites.

EGG BOUND: When a hen is unable to complete egg formation and laying the egg and retains the egg in the oviduct.

FEATHER PICKING: An unwanted and detrimental action when chickens pick and pull at each other's feathers. This behavior often starts from stress, aggression, or nutritional issues in a flock.

FLEDGE: To care for young birds that are still in the nest.

GALLUS DOMESTICUS: The scientific name for a domestic chicken.

GIZZARD: An internal chicken organ that crushes food with the help of pebbles or grit.

GRIT: Pebbles, oyster shell or sand used by chickens to break down ingested food.

GROWER FEED: A feed formulated for growing chickens, usually used for nine to twenty weeks.

GROWERS: Chickens aged between the end of brooding and sexual maturity.

HACKLES: These are the long feathers on a chicken's neck. Males have thin, pointed feathers and females have thick, rounded feathers.

HEN: A female chicken one year of age or older.

HOCK: The joint between the thigh and the shank, where the feathered portion of the leg ends and the scaly shank of the lower leg begins.

INCUBATION: A process used to hatch eggs. Incubation can happen naturally by chickens sitting on eggs or artificially with a mechanical incubator.

LAYER CYCLE: This is the period from the onset of laying until molting causes the hen to stop laying. Layer cycle describes when an economic level of production is maintained.

LAYERS: Female chickens kept for egg production. These are also known as laying hens.

LAYING FEED: Feed formulated with extra calcium for laying hens.

LITTER: Bedding material spread on the floor of a chicken house–straw, wood shavings, etc.

MAREK'S DISEASE: A common viral disease that can be prevented via a vaccination administered to baby chicks.

MOLT: When chickens shed their old feathers and grow new.

MUFF: This is the group of feathers under the chicken's beak that grow out to the sides. Don't confuse it with the beard. Some chickens have a muff, and others a beard, and some have both. Faverolles and Araucanas have muffs.

NEST BOX: A box filled with litter where hens can rest and lay eggs.

NEWCASTLE DISEASE: Because it's a viral respiratory disease, Newcastle disease can spread very quickly. It's prevented by vaccine.

NON-SETTER: Hens that have little or no desire to incubate eggs.

ORNAMENTAL BREED: A breed of chicken used for ornamental purposes. They're appreciated for their beauty rather than for their egg or meat production.

PASTING: Fecal matter stuck on the bird's vent, sealing it close. If not treated, this condition is fatal.

PECKING ORDER: The social organization of a flock from most to least dominant members of the flock.

PIPPING: When baby chicks break open the eggshell and hatch.

PLUME FEATHERS: Soft, downy feathers that are at the base of the shaft, lower thighs and abdomen.

PREEN GLAND: Located at the base of the tail, the preen gland produces a special substance that conditions the feathers.

PRIMARY FEATHERS: The large, stiff feathers on chicken's wings that help them fly. Also known as the wing feathers.

PULLET: A chicken less than a year old.

QUILL: The hollow shaft where the chicken's feather is attached to the body.

ROOSTER: A male chicken that's a year old or more.

ROOST: A perch inside a coop where chickens can rest off the floor.

RUN: An enclosed outdoor area connected to a coop that lets chickens roam freely.

SADDLE FEATHERS: Long, pointed plumage located at the base of the tail feathers. These are prominent on males, less so on females.

SCALES: The hard, overlapping plates on a chicken's feet.

SCRATCH: A type of feed that is usually made of cracked corn and other types of whole grain. It's fed as a treat for backyard chickens.

SECONDARY FEATHERS: These are longer wing feathers that grow from the middle section, and exposed when the wing is folded under.

SEXING: When baby chicks are separated by their gender.

SHAFT: The extension of the qull that runs through the entire length of the feather.

SHANKS: The part of the chicken's legs that's just above the foot.

SPENT HEN: A laying hen that's reached the end of her egg laying life.

SPUR: The horny projection on the rear of a chicken's shank. It's prominent in males and used for defense. The spur grows throughout the birds' life.

STARTER FEED: Pre-mixed food for chicks. Starter feed should be fed to chicks for the first six- to-eight weeks of life. You can buy medicated and non-medicated formulas.

UNTHRIFTY: A term used when raising chickens to describe unhealthy birds that are failing to thrive.

VENT: The opening in the backside of a chicken where waste is eliminated and eggs are laid. Also known as the cloaca.

WASTING: A disease that causes progressive weakness, regression of comb, paleness, enlarged abdomen, emaciation and death.

WATTLE: Thin growths of flesh located on each side of the throat or beak. They are typically red and are usually larger in males.

CHAPTER TWELVE

EQUIPMENT CHECKLIST

Here's a handy-dandy list of the equipment you'll need to raise chickens! Remember, you want to have everything in place *before* you get your chickens home.

For Adult Chickens:

- A chicken house
- Chicken waterers
- Chicken feeders
- Roosts
- Litter
- Nesting boxes
- Secure containers for food and snacks
- Food scoops
- A shovel
- Wheelbarrow
- Small shovel or cat litter scoop
- Rake
- Paint scraper

- Muck Bucket for chicken poop
- Broom
- Basket or bucket for egg collecting
- Egg-count journal
- Thermometer
- Small feed bucket
- Dust masks
- White vinegar
- Scrub brush
- Feed
- Snacks of your choice
- Hen house heater (if necessary)
- Any supplements you'd like to add
- Grit
- Diatomaceous earth

If You Plan On Raising Chicks:

- Brooder
- Litter
- Heater
- Food dish they can't poop in
- Water dish they can't poop in
- Chicken starter food (either medicated or non-medicated)

If You Plan On Hatching Eggs:

- Fertile chicken eggs

- A light source to determine if the eggs are fertile (LED flashlight)
- Incubator
- Brooder (see "If You Plan On Raising Chicks)

Additional Helpful Items:

- Fishing net–If some of your chickens aren't friendly enough to pick up, you can catch them with a fishing net. Just be sure to be careful when you're taking them out so feet and wings don't get caught.
- Rat traps–for obvious reasons
- A live trap for larger animals. Just be sure you have a plan for getting rid of the varmints once you catch them, especially skunks!
- Scissors–for opening bags, etc., but also for clipping wings
- Zip ties and duct tape to make coop repairs on the fly

FINAL WORDS

While there's definitely a bit of a learning curve to raising chickens, remember that you don't have to do everything outlined in this book. Take things at your own pace. There's no need to hatch your own eggs and raise your own chicks, build your own coop or slaughter your own chickens.

Come up with a plan that suits your lifestyle. You can buy, rather than make, everything you need, and there are automatic feeders and waterers if you're unable to get to the chickens at feeding time.

Just in case you're still on the fence, here are some great reasons to own chickens, from naturallvingideas.com:

1. **Fresh eggs:** This is the most obvious reason. Not only are they delicious, you can eat them with a sense of accomplishment!
2. **Organic and non-GMO:** If organic eggs and non-GMO feed are things you're concerned about, it's easy to make that happen. You'll know exactly what your hens are eating and you can avoid feeding them things like antibiotics and engineered grain.
3. **More nutrition:** Free-range eggs from your backyard coop have more than seven times

the Vitamin A and Beta Carotene and almost double the Vitamin E in free range eggs. As for Omega 3 fatty acid, the free range eggs win with 292mg, versus 0.033mg in commercial eggs. Even if your chickens don't roam your entire property, having a large run and feeding them snacks and supplements make for superior eggs.

4. **Cruelty free:** You will know that your chickens were raised humanely, in uncrowded conditions.
5. **You can save a life:** If you're so inclined, and have some experience under your belt, you can rescue factory hens from being slaughtered when their egg production slows a bit. These chickens can be considered "special needs" and require additional care.
6. **Free fertilizer:** Did you know that having between five and 10 chickens should make enough fertilizer for your vegetable garden for a year?
7. **Pest control:** Chickens will eat almost any bug, including slugs, ticks, grasshoppers, and beetles.
8. **Reduce food waste:** As you read, one of Andre's initial reasons for keeping chickens was to feed them the food scraps from his family. They like fruit and vegetable peelings,

bread, cooked starches and pretty much anything. Just avoid animal products.

9. **Save heritage breeds:** Remember reading about the Jersey Giant? It was almost extinct and backyard chicken keepers kept it going. Add some heritage breeds to your flock!
10. **Weed control:** As chickens scratch the ground, they eat the weeds.You'll notice the difference the following spring when you have far fewer weeds to pluck!
11. **Therapy chickens:** When you think of therapy animals, you think of cats and dogs, but chickens are being used as well. They are particularly good for children on the Autism spectrum –it gets them involved in caring for the chickens.
12. **Community:** Be part of something larger than yourself and join a group of fellow backyard chicken raisers. There are plenty of online groups, and you can even find local communities. It's a great way to pick up tips, and show off your own chicken family.
13. **Educational:** If you have children, having them help with the chickens teaches them where food comes from and a sense of responsibility.
14. **It's inexpensive:** There are initial set-up costs, but once you have things up and

running, chickens aren't that expensive to keep.

15. **You can sell eggs:** Excess eggs? Advertise on a local online bulletin board or forum and sell them! Those unfortunate people who don't have their own backyard chickens flock (pardon the pun!) to fresh, local eggs.
16. **Chickens are fun:** Backyard chicken owners love to watch their girls scratch, run around and listen to the noises they make. And, some can be picked up and petted. Remember, they all have their own personalities, so enjoy!

As you can see, there are many good reasons to raise chickens, and perhaps you have some of your own that aren't listed here. Whatever the reason you decide to keep chickens, I wish you the best of luck! May your chickens lay prolifically!

www.ingramcontent.com/pod-product-compliance
Ingram Content Group UK Ltd.
Pitfield, Milton Keynes, MK11 3LW, UK
UKHW020417250726
13967UKWH00007B/2687

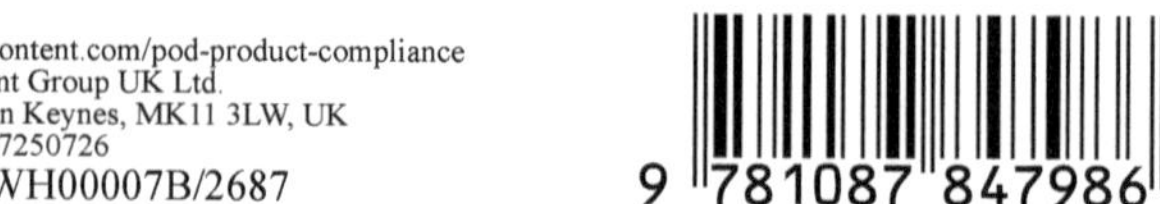

9 781087 847986